BEI GRIN MACHT SICH I
WISSEN BEZAHLT

- Wir veröffentlichen Ihre Hausarbeit,
  Bachelor- und Masterarbeit

- Ihr eigenes eBook und Buch -
  weltweit in allen wichtigen Shops

- Verdienen Sie an jedem Verkauf

Jetzt bei www.GRIN.com hochladen und kostenlos publizieren

Bibliografische Information der Deutschen Nationalbibliothek:

Die Deutsche Bibliothek verzeichnet diese Publikation in der Deutschen National-bibliografie; detaillierte bibliografische Daten sind im Internet über http://dnb.d-nb.de/ abrufbar.

Impressum:

Copyright © 2019 GRIN Verlag
Druck und Bindung: Books on Demand GmbH, Norderstedt Germany
ISBN: 9783346174963

Dieses Buch bei GRIN:

https://www.grin.com/document/537641

Sophia von Lingen

Soziale Ungleichheit und Prozesse der Statusbildung anhand der Methode "Schritt nach Vorne"

GRIN Verlag

Universität zu Köln

Humanwissenschaftliche Fakultät

Seminar: Interkulturelle Didaktik

Hausarbeit zum Thema:

Prozesse der Statusbildung am Beispiel der Übung „Schritt nach Vorn"

Vorgelegt von:

Sophia von Lingen

Abgabe: 31.03.2019

Inhalt

Anmerkung der Redaktion: Der Anhang ist aus urheberrechtlichen Gründen nicht Teil der Veröffentlichung

1. Einleitung:

„Alle sind gleich, doch manche sind gleicher als andere. In dieser Übung erfahren die Teilnehmenden, wie es in ihrer Gesellschaft ist, ‚anders‘ zu sein." (Brander 2005, S. 132) Diese Beschreibung wurde von Brander für die Übung „Schritt nach Vorn" gewählt und verweist auf zweierlei.

Zunächst gibt es den Verweis darauf, was es bedeutet in einer Gesellschaft „anders" zu sein. Diese Frage führt zu weiteren Fragen: „Anders als wer? Und welche Determinanten sorgen dafür, dass ich anders bin oder anders gemacht werde?" Der Frage nach dem Anders-Sein soll sich der erste Teil dieser Arbeit widmen. Dazu sollen zunächst exemplarisch Möglichkeiten der Humandifferenzierung vorgestellt werden. Danach wird die Bedeutung dieser Kategorisierung für die Herstellung von Ordnung und Verortung herausgearbeitet, welche Grundlage dafür ist, warum aus zunächst neutralen Unterscheidungen Determinanten sozialer Ungleichheit werden. Dies verweist auf den ersten Teil des Zitats „Alle sind gleich, doch manche sind gleicher als andere".

Die sozialwissenschaftliche und politische Auseinandersetzung in Bezug auf soziale Ungleichheit und Diskriminierung lassen sich darin zusammenfassen, dass es eine deutliche Diskrepanz gibt zwischen dem Selbstverständnis moderner Gesellschaften, die in Anlehnung an aufklärerische Gedanken aus freien und gleichen Individuen besteht und der Realität ungleicher Lebensbedingungen und Lebenschancen (vgl. Scherr 2014, S. 1).

Im zweiten Theorieblock soll sich darum an das Phänomen der sozialen Ungleichheit angenähert werden. Nach einer begrifflichen Bestimmung werden die Basisdimensionen der sozialen Ungleichheit vorgestellt. Die Ergebnisse der beiden Theorieblöcke werden systematisiert und mit dem Prinzip der Statusbildung verknüpft.

Nach der theoretischen Auseinandersetzung wird die Methode „Schritt nach Vorn" vorgestellt und nach dem oben genannten Prinzip von Aspekten der Kategorisierung dem ungleichen Zugang zu wertvollen Gütern und deren Zusammenwirken analysiert. Dies soll dem vorangestellten Prinzip als Veranschaulichung dienen. Dabei soll die Frage beantwortet werden, wie es im Verlauf der Methode zu einer heterogenen Statusverteilung kommt. Im Fazit wird darüber hinaus noch auf das Potential und die Schwierigkeiten der Übung eingegangen.

2. Humandifferenzierung und Kategorisierung

Hirschauer unterscheidet kulturelle Phänomene im Gegensatz zu naturhaft gegebenen Unterschieden darin, dass sie aus „kontingenten sinnhaften *Unterscheidungen* bestehen, die von historisch und geografisch spezifischen Kontexten geprägt sind." (Hirschauer 2014, S. 170).

Die Unterscheidungen können wie beim Geschlecht oder beim Alter an quasi-biologische Merkmale anknüpfen oder können auch von vornherein menschengemachte Kategorien sein, wie der Beruf oder die ethnische Zugehörigkeit (vgl. Hradil 2001, 34 f.). Der erste Teil der Arbeit soll sich mit den wichtigsten dieser Differenzierungen auseinandersetzen: Mit jenen, mit denen sich die Unterscheider selbst voneinander unterscheiden. Diese markieren soziale Zugehörigkeiten, bestimmen über die Zusammensetzung von Gruppen, schreiben Individuen Mitgliedschaften zu und subjektivieren sie in spezifischen kulturellen Kategorien (vgl. Hirschauer 2014, S. 170). Diese, im Alltag als „individuelle Eigenschaften" wahrgenommen Effekte werden soziologisch als Mitgliedschaften gefasst, die auf den *Zugehörigkeiten zu Kollektiven* beruhen (vgl. ebd.). Die Wahrnehmung von Individualität ist daher als Resultat aus vielfältigen, heterogenen Zugehörigkeiten zu Kollektiven zu verstehen.

2.1. Arten der Kategorisierungen

Die sozialwissenschaftliche Beobachtung zeigt, dass es eine enorme Heterogenität und Varianz von Kategorisierungen gibt, die Grundlage von Humandifferenzierung sind (vgl. Hirschauer 2014, S. 171). Neben den traditionsreichen kulturgeschichtlichen Kategorisierungen wie Alter und Geschlecht gibt es stratifikatorische Differenzierungen wie Klassen und Statusgruppen sowie Unterscheidungen in Bezug auf Generationen, Milieus und Berufsgruppen, aber auch Differenzierungen nach Dialekt oder Attraktivität (vgl. Hirschauer 2014, S. 171)[1]. Exemplarisch seien an dieser Stelle einige entscheidende Leitdifferenzen vorgestellt.

Die *Geschlechtsdifferenz* ist eine der ältesten Formen der Humandifferenzierung. Dabei handelt es sich meist um eine binäre Kategorisierung. Neben der biologischen Unterscheidung, die als „natürliche Unterscheidung"[2] (Sex) zu verstehen ist, gibt es auch das soziale Geschlecht (Gender), welches die Individuen mit geschlechtsspezifischen Zuschreibungen und damit mit essenzieller Verschiedenartigkeit ausstattet. Kessler/McKenna (1978) sprechen in diesem Zusammenhang auch von „kulturellen Genitalien". *Ethnizität* ist als imaginierte Zugehörigkeit zu einer Gemeinschaft zu verstehen, deren Mitglieder an eine Vorstellung von gemeinsamer Kultur und Abstammung glauben. Diese Vorstellung beruht bspw. auf kulturellen Praktiken,

---

[1] Auf eine nähere Ausführung zur Schicht, Klassen und Milieu-Unterscheidung wird an dieser Stelle verzichtet. Dazu sei auf den Beitrag von Stefan Hradil in „soziale Ungleichheit in Deutschland hingewiesen (2001, S. 36 – 46).
[2] Auch beim biologischen Geschlecht sind die Differenzen nicht immer eindeutig. Siehe dazu auch: Meuser 2010 „Geschlechtersoziologie"

Ursprungsmythen oder körperlichen Ähnlichkeiten (vgl. Hirschauer 2014, S. 171). *Religiöse Zugehörigkeit* beruft sich nicht nur auf Gemeinsamkeitsvorstellungen, sondern setzt an einem gemeinsamen Glauben, bzw. an gemeinsamen Überzeugungen, an. Diese können der Veränderung unterworfen sein (vgl. ebd.). *Nationale Differenzierung* verbindet die „vorgestellte Gemeinschaft" mit einem Anspruch auf politisch-territoriale Souveränität. Kollektividentitäten sollen hierbei an ein staatliches Bewusstsein geknüpft werden, welches zwischen Einheimischen und Ausländern unterscheidet (vgl. ebd.). In der Unterscheidung von *„Normalität und Devianz"* findet sich die Kategorisierung der *Kriminalität*, die als abweichendes Verhalten von Normen und im Sinne des ‚labeling approach' als soziale Zuschreibung verstanden wird (Hess und Scheerer 2014, S. 17–46). Auch *Gesundheit und Krankheit* sind als Differenzkategorie zu betrachten. Die Vorstellung von Krankheit und Körper ist dabei als gewachsene gesellschaftliche Konstruktion zu verstehen (vgl. Hanses und Richter 2011, S. 137). Dies hat insbesondere Foucault (1976) in seiner Analyse des „klinischen Blicks" herausgearbeitet.

Leistung unterscheidet sich von den bisher genannten Kategorisierung darin, dass diese gerade in kapitalistischen Systemen als „sozialer Gleichmacher" fungieren soll, der von Unterscheidungen askriptiver und kategorialer Art absehen soll (Hirschauer 2014, S. 171). Die objektive Leistungsmessung soll als sozial neutraler Akt zu verstehen sein (vgl. ebd.).

Bei einigen dieser Kategorisierungen und Mitgliedschaften haben die Einzelnen wenig Einflussmöglichkeiten auf die Zugehörigkeit, wie beim Alter oder beim Geschlecht, weshalb sie als „zugeschriebene" Kategorisierungen bezeichnet werden. Andere Determinanten, wie der Beruf oder die religiöse Zugehörigkeit kann das Individuum durch eigenes Zutun erwerben oder verändern (vgl. Hradil 2001, S. 35). Ob eine Kategorie veränderbar ist, kann jedoch auch, wie bei der religiösen Zugehörigkeit von Gesellschaft zu Gesellschaft verschieden sein (vgl. ebd.). Einige Differenzierungen setzen an den Körpern an, andere an Tätigkeiten oder Gütern. Einige werden als konstant erwartet, andere (wie das Alter) sind transitorisch (vgl. Hirschauer 2014, S. 171). Einige beziehen sich auf die Herstellung von Individuen (Leistung), andere auf Kollektive (Ethnizität) (vgl. ebd.).

Im Rahmen dieser Mitgliedschaften und Kategorisierungen sind selbstverständlich auch Mehrfachzugehörigkeiten möglich. Studien zur Intersektionalität beziehen sich auf das Zusammenspiel von bestimmten Differenzkategorien, wie zum Beispiel der Ethnizität und dem Geschlecht (Hirschauer 2014, S. 175).

2.2. Die Bedeutungen von Kategorisierungen

„(...) klassifizieren heißt, der Welt eine Struktur zu geben (...)." (Bauman 1992, S. 14). Es scheint so etwas wie einen kulturellen Ordnungsbedarf zu geben, der nach Aufrechterhaltung von Kategorien strebt, um Orientierungs- und Handlungssicherheit zu gewährleisten (vgl. Hirschauer 2014, S. 173). Dieser Prozess der Ordnungskonstruktion durch kulturelle Kategorien wird nach Bauman von zwei Funktionen angetrieben: Die Bannung desorientierender Ambiguität zugunsten von Ordnung und zum anderen die Selbstverortung des Unterscheiders, welcher sich mit der Identifizierung eines imaginären oder realen „Anderen" seiner selbst vergewissert und sich verortet (vgl. Bauman 1992). Mit der Unterscheidung von verschiedenen „Menschensorten" kommt es zu verschiedenen Formen von Asymmetrien, die mit der Funktion der Selbstverortung einhergehen (vgl. Hirschauer 2014, S. 173). Denn es gibt bei Unterscheidungen zwischen Menschen keinen neutralen Betrachter, vielmehr wird die Unterscheidung immer von irgendwem und irgendwo vollzogen. Die Unterscheidung platziert den Unterscheidenden selbst wie bei „hier und dort" auf eine Seite (vgl. Hirschauer 2014, S. 174). Daraus gehen Prozesse der Integration und Abgrenzung hervor, die von leichten Präferenzen für die „ingroup" bis zu ausgeprägten Formen von Auf- und Abwertungen reichen (vgl. ebd.).

3. Kategorisierungen als Determinanten sozialer Ungleichheiten

Daraus resultiert auch, dass Menschen im Vergleich miteinander nicht einfach, wie im vorangegangenen beschrieben wurde, als unterschiedlich und in bestimmter Hinsicht als verschiedenartig charakterisiert werden, sondern dass mit dieser Positionierung eine Hierarchisierung als Besser- oder Schlechter-, Höher- oder Tieferstellung entsteht (vgl. Hradil 2001, S. 27). Solche Kategorisierungen, die mit einer Hierarchisierung einhergehen, werden als Erscheinungen sozialer Ungleichheit verstanden (vgl. ebd.).

Die Untersuchung von Determinanten sozialer Ungleichheit geht über die reine Beschreibung von Kategorisierungen hinaus. Als Determinanten sozialer Ungleichheit werden jene Kategorisierungen bezeichnet, die nicht per se eine Besser- oder Schlechterstellung darstellen, diese jedoch im Alltag mit hoher Wahrscheinlichkeit nach sich ziehen (wie bspw. das Geschlecht, der Beruf, die Ethnizität) (vgl. Hradil 2001, S. 34). So ist es kein Nachteil, eine Frau zu sein und trotzdem sind mit dem weiblichen Geschlecht in diversen Gesellschaften beträchtliche Nachteile verknüpft, die sich z.B. in schlechteren Berufs- Einkommens- und

Durchsetzungschancen widerspiegeln (vgl. ebd.). Damit wird mit der an sich neutralen Unterscheidung eine Schlechterstellung real wirksam.

3.1. Der Begriff der sozialen Ungleichheit

Der Begriff der sozialen Ungleichheit beinhaltet verschiedene Aspekte. Zunächst bezieht sich der Begriff auf „Güter" die in einer Gesellschaft als besonders „wertvoll" und wünschenswert erachtet werden (vgl. Hradil 2001, S. 28). Je mehr die einzelne Person von diesen Gütern besitzt, desto günstiger sind seine Lebensbedingungen (vgl. ebd.). Unter Lebensbedingungen werden hierbei als „äußere, vom Denken und Verhalten des einzelnen kurzfristig nicht beeinflußbare Rahmenbedingungen des Lebens zu verstehen." (Hradil 2001, S. 28). All diejenigen, die über diese wertvollen Güter verfügen, haben Vorteile denen gegenüber, die diese Güter nicht besitzen, sodass sie gesellschaftlich als besser- oder höhergestellt empfunden werden (vgl. ebd.). „Wertvoll" sind bestimmte Güter dann, wenn sie mit „Vorstellungen vom Wünschenswerten" verbunden sind (Kluckhohn 1951). Um als Erscheinungsform sozialer Ungleichheit in Frage zu kommen, muss der Besitz dieser „Güter" mit der Erlangung von gesellschaftlich erstrebenswert erachteten Zielen verknüpft sein (Bspw. Geld, unkündbare Berufsstellung, Bildung) (vgl. Hradil 2001, S. 28).

Neben der Frage, weshalb bestimmte Güter so wertvoll sind kommt die Frage danach, wie diese Güter verteilt sein müssen, um als „ungleich" zu gelten (vgl. ebd.). In der Soziologie wird von „sozialer Ungleichheit" gesprochen, „wenn als ‚wertvoll' geltende ‚Güter' nicht *absolut gleich verteilt* sind." (Hradil 2001, S. 29). Absolute Ungleichheit besteht, wenn von den „wertvollen" Gütern einer Gesellschaft ein Mitglied mehr als ein anderes erhält (vgl. ebd., S.28). Das bedeutet auch, dass eine „ungleiche" Verteilung der Güter nicht automatisch auch „ungerecht" sein muss.

Soziale Ungleichheit bezieht nur diejenigen „wertvollen" Güter ein, die aufgrund der sozialen Position des Menschen im Beziehungsgefüge auf „regelmäßige Weise (absolut) ungleich verteilt werden" (ebd.). Es werden also nicht alle Formen der Besser- oder Schlechterstellung berücksichtigt, sondern nur jene, die in „gesellschaftlich strukturierter, vergleichsweise beständiger und verallgemeinerbarer Form zur Verteilung kommen" (ebd.). „Natürliche", „individuelle", „momentane" und zufällige Ungleichheiten gelten dementsprechend nicht als soziale Ungleichheiten (vgl. ebd.). Allerdings sind diese Formen der Ungleichheiten häufig mit sozialen, strukturierten Ungleichheiten verschränkt. Um der Komplexität Rechnung zu tragen, müssen diese Formen der Ungleichheit als zwei zu unterscheidende, aber nicht voneinander unabhängige Formen der gesellschaftlichen Hierarchiebildung verstanden werden[3] (vgl. Scherr 2014, S. 2).

Es existieren zwei „Strukturierungsarten" von sozialer Ungleichheit, die sich entweder auf die „strukturierte ungleiche Verteilung ‚wertvoller' Güter *unter allen Betroffenen Menschen schlechthin*" beziehen kann oder sich auf die Ungleichheit „zwischen bestimmten Gruppen innerhalb dieser ungleichen Verteilung" beziehen kann (Hradil 2001, S. 30). Bei der letzten Form werden die oben genannten Kategorisierungen relevant. Besonders bei zugeschriebenen Kategorisierungen (Männer und Frauen, In- und Ausländer), gelten Ungleichheiten als „ungerecht", da sie modernen Vorstellungen von gerechter Verteilung verstärkt widersprechen (Hradil 2001, S. 30). Als zusammenfassende Definition gilt: „,*Soziale Ungleichheit' liegt dann vor, wenn Menschen aufgrund ihrer Stellung in sozialen Beziehungsgefügen von den ‚wertvollen Gütern' einer Gesellschaft regelmäßig mehr als andere erhalten.*" (Hradil 2001, S. 30)

3.2. Dimensionen sozialer Ungleichheit in Korrelation zum „Status"

Stefan Hradil unterscheidet drei „Basisdimensionen" sozialer Ungleichheit, die die Vielfalt der Erscheinungsformen zusammenfassen sollen. Diese sind *Materieller Wohlstand, Macht* und *Prestige* (Hradil 2001, S. 31). Diese erweitern sich spätestens in der postindustriellen „Wissens- und Informationsgesellschaft" um die Dimension der *Bildung*. Diese Dimensionen sind von entscheidender Bedeutung, wenn es um die Verwirklichung gesellschaftlicher Wertvorstellungen eines „guten Lebens" geht (vgl. ebd.). Diese Dimensionen sind rein logisch unabhängig voneinander. Empirisch zeigt sich jedoch, dass Vor – oder Nachteile in einem der Bereiche sich auch auf andere Bereiche übertragen (können) (vgl. ebd.). Soziale Ungleichheiten werden in ihrer Bedeutung erst dann verständlich, wenn die Konsequenzen im privaten und öffentlichen Leben mitberücksichtigt werden. Materieller Wohlstand wirkt sich demnach nicht nur auf die Geldmenge, sondern auch in Graden der Freiheit, der Kontakte, des Selbstbewusstseins etc. aus. Nur so wird die Besserstellung wohlhabender Menschen vollends deutlich (vgl. ebd., S. 32). Die (bessere oder schlechtere) Stellung in einer Gesellschaft bezogen auf die Dimensionen der sozialen Ungleichheit wird als „Status" bezeichnet (vgl. ebd., 33). Die Zuordnungen des Einzelnen auf verschiedenen Ebenen der Dimensionen wird *„Statusverteilung"* genannt (vgl. ebd.). Menschen mit ähnlich hohem Status werden als

---

[3] So ist die Lage eines Behinderten nur unter der Berücksichtigung von sowohl natürlichen bzw. individuellen als auch sozialen Ungleichheiten zu erkennen (vgl. Hradil 2001, 30).

„Statusgruppe" zusammengefasst (vgl. ebd.). Ist der Status eines Menschen in verschiedenen Dimensionen einheitlich, wird von *„Statuskonsistenz"* gesprochen (vgl. ebd.). Wenn es starke Abweichungen im Status der unterschiedlichen Dimensionen gibt, wird von *„Statusinkonsistenz"* gesprochen.

4. systematische Zusammenfassung

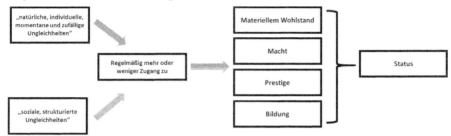

Abbildung 1: Zusammenwirken von Kategorisierungen und Zugang zu Ressourcen auf den Status einer Person.

Die im ersten Teil benannten Aspekte der Humandifferenzierung finden Eingang sowohl auf der Ebene von den „natürlichen, individuellen, momentanen und zufälligen Ungleichheiten", bspw. in Form einer Behinderung oder individuellen Eigenheiten, die als Devianz zur Norm wahrgenommen werden. Vor allem aber finden sie Eingang in die sozialen, strukturierten Ungleichheiten in Form von Besser- oder Schlechter- Stellungen aufgrund des Alters, des Geschlechts oder der Ethnizität, die dazu führen, dass Personen oder Gruppen aufgrund bestimmter Kategorisierungen regelmäßig mehr oder weniger von den „wertvollen" Gütern (materiellem Wohlstand, Macht, Prestige, Bildung) erhalten als andere. Es sind demnach zwei Ebenen zu unterscheiden. Die erste Ebene ist die der Kategorisierung aufgrund bestimmter Merkmale, die auf der zweiten Ebene aufgrund des leichteren oder schwereren Zugangs zu wertvollen Gütern zu einer Besser- oder Schlechterstellung werden. Der Begriff des Status wird demzufolge definiert als „das Zusammenwirken von Kategorisierungen und dem damit einhergehenden Zugang zu „wertvollen" Gütern." Der Status wiederum wird im Sinne der Selbstverortung zum wesentlichen Merkmal einer Person im Beziehungsgefüge.

5. Methode: Schritt nach Vorn

Die Methode Schritt nach Vorn ist eine Methode der Antidiskriminierungspädagogik. Die für die Übung eingesetzten Materialien stammen aus dem Handbuch „Kompass: Handbuch zur Menschenrechtsbildung für die schulische und außerschulische Bildungsarbeit" (Brander 2005,

S. 132–136). Ziel der Übung ist nach Angaben von Brander die „Förderung von Empathie mit Menschen, die nicht zur Mehrheitsgesellschaft gehören, die Sensibilisierung für die ungleiche Chancenverteilung in der Gesellschaft und ein Verständnis für die möglichen persönlichen Folgen der Zugehörigkeit zu bestimmten sozialen Minderheiten zu wecken." (Brander 2005, S. 132). Dazu werden zunächst Rollenkarten an die Teilnehmenden verteilt[4]. Die Teilnehmenden werden gebeten, sich durch gezielte Fragestellungen in die Lage ihrer Rolle hineinzuversetzen. Beispiele für solche Fragen könnten sein: Wie war deine Kindheit? Konntest du viel draußen spielen oder hast du eher drinnen gespielt? In was für einem Haus hast du gewohnt? Welchen Beruf hatten oder haben deine Eltern? Wie sieht dein Alltag aus? Hast du einen festen Job? Wie sieht dein Lebensstil aus? Was machst du in deiner Freizeit? Wie viel Geld verdienst du? Was findest du aufregend und wovor fürchtest du dich? (vgl. Brander 2005, S. 135). Die Teilnehmenden werden gebeten, sich an einer Linie aufzustellen. Danach werden bestimmte Situationen und Ereignisse vorgelesen[5]. Wenn die Teilnehmenden die Frage mit „Ja" beantworten, gehen sie einen Schritt nach Vorn. Wenn nicht, bleiben sie einfach stehen. Ob die Teilnehmenden eine Frage bezogen auf ihre Rolle mit „Ja" oder „Nein" beantworten, liegt in ihrem eigenen ermessen. Es gibt somit keine „falschen" oder „richtigen" Antworten. Dadurch entsteht am Ende eine Differenz zwischen Personen, die bei fast jeder Frage einen Schritt nach Vorn gegangen sind und anderen, die noch an der Startlinie stehen oder nur wenige Schritte nach vorn gegangen sind.

5.1. Analyse der Methode

Die Qualität dieser Arbeit soll darin liegen, auf Basis der vorangegangenen Herleitung vom Status, im Verständnis vom „Zusammenwirken von Kategorisierungen und dem Zugang zu „wertvollen" Gütern zu erklären, warum es am Ende der Methode zu einer solchen heterogen gestreuten Statusverteilung kommt und welche Qualität dieser Prozess hat.

Dazu werden drei Analyseschritte durchgeführt. Der erste Schritt bezieht sich auf die Analyse der Rollen und ihrer zugehörigen Kategorisierungen. Der zweite Analyseschritt bezieht sich auf die Situationen und Ereignisse, die mit einem bestimmten Zugang zu „wertvollen" Gütern verbunden sind. Zuletzt sollen die Erkenntnisse und die Beziehungen der einzelnen Abschnitte zueinander herausgearbeitet werden.

---

[4] Die Beschreibung der Rollen findet sich im Anhang unter A1.
[5] Die Situationen und Ereignisse finden sich im Anhang unter A2.

5.1.1. Analyse der Kategorisierungen

Im Folgenden soll nachvollzogen werden, welche Prozesse die Teilnehmenden durchlaufen, um schließlich eine Frage entweder mit „Ja" oder mit „Nein" zu beantworten. Dazu wurden nach dem Zufallsprinzip sechs von den zwanzig Rollenkarten ausgewählt. Die Rollenkarten enthalten unterschiedlich viele Informationen über die Rolle, sodass ein gewisser Imaginationsspielraum immer besteht. Dennoch geben die Rollen eine Grundlage, die eine Kategorisierung, wie sie im ersten Teil beschrieben wurde, ermöglicht. Diese Kategorisierungen anhand der Informationen soll in der folgenden Tabelle vorgenommen werden. Dabei werden auch im Sinne der Intersektionalität die Mehrfachzugehörigkeiten zu Kategorisierungen deutlich. Diese Tabelle soll nur eine der vielen Möglichkeiten darstellen, wie eine solche Kategorisierung bei den einzelnen Teilnehmenden aussehen kann.

Tabelle 1: Möglichkeiten der Humandifferenzierung

Rollenbeschreibung	Kategorisierung
Sie sind die Tochter des örtlichen Bankdirektors. Sie studieren Wirtschaftswissenschaften an der Universität.	Geschlecht, Alter, Leistung, Berufsperspektive
Sie sind ein behinderter junger Mann, der an den Rollstuhl gefesselt ist.	Krankheit, Alter, Geschlecht
Sie sind ein illegaler Einwanderer aus Mali.	Geschlecht, Ethnizität, Kriminalität, Hautfarbe
Sie sind Inhaberin einer erfolgreichen Import-Export-Firma.	Geschlecht, Beruf
Sie sind ein arbeitsloser Lehrer in einem Land, dessen neue Amtssprache Sie nicht fließend beherrschen.	Geschlecht, Ethnizität, Beruf
Sie sind 22 Jahre alt und lesbisch	Alter, Geschlecht, sexuelle Orientierung

Die hier vorgenommene Einteilung stellt eine Reduktion dar, die dem Selbstverständnis der einzelnen Rollen widersprechen kann, entspricht jedoch demselben Reduktionsprozess, den auch die Teilnehmenden zu Beginn der Methode vornehmen. Damit geht auch die Gefahr einher, die Mitgliedschaften wieder zu sozialen Eigenschaften von Individuen zu reifizieren. Daher ist im Blick zu behalten, dass es sich hier primär um Eigenschaften der Sozialorganisation handelt (vgl. Hirschauer 2014, S. 172).

5.1.2. Analyse der Situationen und Ereignisse

In einem zweiten Analyseschritt wird versucht, die gestellten Situationen und Ereignisse auf die Basisdimensionen der sozialen Ungleichheit „materielle Ressourcen, Macht, Prestige und Bildung" aufzuteilen. Dabei wird nicht berücksichtigt, dass einige Situationen und Ereignisse durchaus mehrere Aspekte beinhalten können. So kann „Sie können an einem internationalen Seminar im Ausland teilnehmen" sich sowohl auf die Bildung beziehen, weil mit der Teilnahme an einem internationalen Seminar der Zugang zu Bildung entweder verwehrt oder ermöglicht wird, als auch auf die materiellen Ressourcen beziehen, mit der Frage danach, ob die notwendigen finanziellen Mittel für eine solche Auslandsreise zur Verfügung stehen. Damit lässt sich auch die Konvertierbarkeit der Dimensionen aufzeigen. Die vorliegende Einordnung ist mit einem dementsprechenden Augenmaß zu bewerten und stellt eine Vereinfachung dar.

Tabelle 2: Einteilung der Situationen und Ereignisse auf die "wertvollen" Güter.

Materielle Ressourcen	Macht	Prestige	Bildung
Sie haben nie in ernsthaften finanziellen Schwierigkeiten gesteckt.	Sie haben das Gefühl, dass Ihre Meinung über soziale und politische Fragen eine Rolle spielt und dass man Ihnen zuhört.	Sie haben das Gefühl, dass Ihre Sprache, Religion und Kultur in der Gesellschaft, in der Sie leben, respektiert werden.	Sie haben das Gefühl, Sie können studieren und Ihren Wunschberuf ergreifen.
Sie leben in einem bescheidenen Haus mit Telefon und Fernsehen.	Andere Menschen holen zu verschiedenen Problemen Ihren Rat ein.	Sie haben keine Angst, in eine Polizeikontrolle zu geraten.	Sie können an einem internationalen Seminar im Ausland teilnehmen.
Sie können einmal im Jahr verreisen und Urlaub machen.	Sie können bei nationalen und kommunalen Wahlen Ihre Stimme abgeben.	Sie hatten nie das Gefühl, dass Sie aufgrund Ihrer Herkunft diskriminiert werden.	
Sie können Freunde und Freundinnen nach Hause zum Essen einladen.	Sie wissen, wohin Sie sich wenden können, wenn Sie Rat und Hilfe brauchen.	Sie haben keine Angst, auf der Straße oder in den Medien belästigt oder angegriffen zu werden.	
Sie können mindestens einmal pro Woche ins Kino oder ins Theater gehen.	Sie haben das Gefühl, dass Ihr Wissen und Ihre Fähigkeiten in der Gesellschaft, in der Sie leben, anerkannt sind	Sie können die wichtigsten religiösen Feste mit Ihren Verwandten, Freunden und Freundinnen feiern.	
Sie können mindestens alle drei Monate einmal neue Sachen zum Anziehen kaufen.		Sie können sich verlieben, in wen Sie wollen.	
Sie haben Zugang zum Internet und profitieren davon.			

Ihre sozialen und medizinischen Bedürfnisse werden ausreichend abgedeckt.			
Sie haben ein interessantes Leben und sind zuversichtlich, was Ihre Zukunft betrifft.			
Sie haben keine Angst um die Zukunft Ihrer Kinder.			

Die Aussagen „Sie haben ein interessantes Leben und sind zuversichtlich, was ihre Zukunft betrifft" und „Sie haben keine Angst um die Zukunft ihrer Kinder" bezieht sich im Gegensatz zu den anderen Situationen und Ereignissen auf Zukunftsaussichten und sind als Konglomerat aus allen Bereichen zu verstehen.

5.1.3. Zusammenwirken von Kategorisierungen und Zugang zu wertvollen Gütern

Es stellt sich die Frage, weshalb sich die Teilnehmenden dafür entscheiden, einen Schritt nach Vorn zu gehen oder nicht und warum sich am Ende dadurch eine sehr breit gefächerte Streuung unter den Teilnehmenden über den Raum ergibt.

Die Teilnehmenden bekommen ihre Rollenkarte zugeteilt und bewusst oder unbewusst wird diese Rolle mit Kategorisierungen verknüpft. Diese Kategorisierung an sich stellt jedoch noch keine Besser- oder Schlechterstellung im Sinne einer sozialen Ungleichheit dar, denn damit sind zunächst keine Chancen oder Begrenzungen verknüpft. In der Methode wird dies dadurch deutlich, dass alle Teilnehmenden auf derselben Linie starten. Um den Prozess der Statusverteilung nachvollziehen zu können, muss bewusst sein, dass die Kategorisierungen die Grundlage darstellen, aufgrund derer die Teilnehmenden eine Bewertung vornehmen.

„Sie sind ein arbeitsloser Lehrer in einem Land, dessen neue Amtssprache Sie nicht fließend beherrschen." - als Kategorisierungen liegen dabei einerseits der Beruf, aber auch die Arbeitslosigkeit, das Geschlecht und die Ethnizität zu Grunde. Dazu wird die Situation „Sie haben nie in ernsthaften finanziellen Schwierigkeiten gesteckt" vorgelesen. Um diese Frage aus der Rolle heraus beantworten zu können, werden die vorhandenen Kategorisierungen mit dem Ereignis verglichen und bewertet. In dem Fall ist es wahrscheinlich, dass von der Arbeitslosigkeit auf finanzielle Schwierigkeiten geschlossen wird, die am Ende dazu führen, dass der/ die Teilnehmer*in eher stehen bleiben wird, als einen Schritt nach Vorn zu gehen. Bei der Rollenkarte: „Sie sind 22 Jahre alt und lesbisch" findet sich keine Kategorisierung, die es erlauben würde, auf den Zugang zu materiellen Ressourcen zu schließen. In diesem Fall ist es der/ dem Teilnehmenden völlig freigestellt, die eigene Rollenimagination zu nutzen und sich für ein „Ja" oder „Nein" zu entscheiden. Bei „Sie sind die Tochter des örtlichen Bankdirektors.

Sie studieren Wirtschaftswissenschaften an der Universität" bietet die Kategorisierung aufgrund der ökonomischen Herkunft die Basis aufgrund derer sich der/ die Teilnehmende vermutlich eher für einen Schritt nach Vorn entscheiden würde. Dabei ist bei dieser Rollenkarte davon auszugehen, dass es sich um einen statuskonsistenten Rollencharakter handelt. Dies lässt sich daran erkennen, dass der Rollenfigur materielle Ressourcen zur Verfügung stehen und Bildungsressourcen zur Verfügung stehen, was sich an einem abgeschlossenen Schulabschluss und dem Studium erkennen lässt. Vermittelt über den Vater sind ebenfalls indirekt Prestige und Macht vorhanden. Bei „Sie sind ein arbeitsloser Lehrer in einem Land, dessen neue Amtssprache Sie nicht fließend beherrschen" würde man von Statusinkonsistenz sprechen, da auf einen Seite zwar von dem Gut Bildung vorhanden ist, diese jedoch nicht in materielle Ressourcen konvertierbar ist und es daher eine große Differenz zwischen den materiellen Ressourcen und den Bildungsressourcen gibt. An dieser Stelle sei auch auf das in Kapitel 2.1. beschriebene Phänomen der Intersektionalität hingewiesen. So handelt es sich bei „Sie sind ein illegaler Einwanderer aus Mali" um ein Zusammenkommen von vielfachen Kategorisierungen, wie Kriminalität, Ethnizität, ggfs. auch Hautfarbe, die in ihrem Zusammenwirken dazu führen werden, dass diese Rolle vermutlich nur wenige Schritte nach Vorn machen wird. Hier sind bereits die Kategorien für sich genommen schon sehr wirkmächtig. Jedoch nur, wenn diese in ihrem Zusammenspiel gesehen werden, können Mechanismen von Mehrfachdiskriminierung nachvollzogen werden, welche sich essenziell auf den Zugang zu wertvollen Gütern auswirken. Aus dem Zusammenwirken von Kategorisierungen und dem indirekten Fragen nach dem Zugang zu wertvollen Gütern, ergibt sich am Ende der „Status" einer Person. Dieser Status ist auch ein räumlicher Status, der sich im Sinne der Selbstverortung aus der Differenz zu den anderen Personen im Raum ergibt. Wenn sich mehrere Teilnehmende auf derselben Höhe befinden, dann kann man von Statusgruppen sprechen. Die räumlichen Positionen und der damit verbundene Status von allen teilnehmenden Rollencharakteren ergibt zum Schluss die Statusverteilung. Spätestens in diesem Moment soll den Teilnehmenden der Zusammenhang zwischen Kategorisierungen und einem ungleichen Zugang zu wertvollen Gütern bewusst werden, die ihren Status im Laufe der Übung maßgeblich beeinflusst haben.

6. Fazit: Potential und Kritik an der Methode Schritt nach Vorn

Die vorangegangenen Erläuterungen zu theoretischen Konzepten von Kategorisierungen und dem ungleichen Zugang zu „wertvollen Gütern" als Grundlage der Statusbildung und die

Verknüpfung mit der praktischen Übung „Schritt nach Vorn" haben gezeigt, wie sehr der Status einer Person durch Kategorisierungen und dem damit verbundenem Zugang zu wertvollen Gütern determiniert wird und im Sinne der Selbstverortung darüber Vorstellungen über die Position in der Gesellschaft geprägt werden. Dies wirkt sich maßgeblich auf das Selbstverständnis und Selbstbewusstsein einer Person aus und prägt dessen Welt- und Selbstverhältnis. Die Methode eignet sich damit, wie im Vorangegangenen deutlich gemacht wurde, um die Prozesse von Kategorisierungen und dem Zugang zu wertvollen Gütern zu veranschaulichen und den Teilnehmenden in einem anschließenden Gespräch zu verdeutlichen oder vielleicht sogar erst bewusst zu machen, welche Mechanismen bei der Herstellung sozialer Ungleichheit wirken. Die Methode kann mit theoretischen Inhalten verknüpft werden und veranschaulicht dadurch Statusphänomene, wie Status(in)konsistenz, Statusgruppen und Statusverteilung. Auch Theorien der Intersektionalität können anhand der Rollenbeschreibungen verdeutlicht werden und die Bedeutung der Selbstverortung kann anhand der Statusverteilung deutlich gemacht werden. Das Potential dieser Übung bezieht sich damit nicht nur auf die in Punkt 5. beschriebenen Hauptlernziele, die sich vorrangig auf die Bewusstwerdung von Verknüpfungen von Kategorisierungen und dem ungleichen Zugang zu wertvollen Gütern beziehen, sondern können auch thematisch mit verwandten Theorien zur Veranschaulichung verknüpft werden.

Dem gegenüber steht auch eine Kritik, die sich aus dem Aufbau der Übung ergibt. Die Teilnehmenden werden im gesamten ersten Teil dazu aufgefordert, sich in die Lage ihrer Rolle hineinzuversetzen. Damit werden ganz massiv innere Bilder aktiviert, die auf Rollenkarten wie „Sie sind eine 17-jährige Sinti und Roma, die die Grundschule nicht besucht hat" oder auch „Sie sind ein illegaler Einwanderer aus Mali" beruhen. Diese aktivieren fundamental medial oder gesellschaftlich produzierte Vorurteile. Diese Übung kann ihr Potential nur dann entfalten, wenn man Kategorisierungen bewusst vornimmt und sich mit stereotypischen Bildern identifiziert. Man provoziert somit stereotype Kategorisierungen mit der Gefahr, bestehende sozial konstruierte Kategorisierungen, wie die der Ethnizität oder Formen der Behinderung zusätzlich zu verstärken. Der Lernerfolg dieser Übung kann nur durch die Aktivierung starker Stereotypen entstehen.

Dazu kommt ein weiterer Punkt: Je nach Gruppe hat man möglicherweise Teilnehmende dabei, die bereits am eigenen Leib die Verbindung von Kategorisierung und einem damit einhergehenden eingeschränkten Zugang zu „wertvollen Gütern" erlebt haben. Diese Teilnehmenden werden durch die Übung noch einmal fiktiv in die Lage versetzt und

„durchleben" im Rahmen dieser Übung sodann, was sie am eigenen Körper bereits erfahren haben. Die Frage stellt sich danach, ob es gerechtfertigt erscheint, den Lernerfolg der Einen zu Lasten von Anderen zu unterstützen. Von Daher müssen das Potential und das Risiko vor der Durchführung der Methode abgewogen werden. Dies beinhaltet das Hinterfragen, ob der Lernerfolg so groß ist, dass die Mittel als zweitrangig zu betrachten sind. Durch Plenumsdiskussionen können zusätzlich bestimmte Aspekte der Übung vorentlastet oder hinterher besprochen werden. Der/ die Moderierende sollte hinterfragen, inwiefern er/sie in der Lage ist, die Verstärkung der Kategorisierung im ersten Teil wieder auffangen zu können, sodass am Ende nicht der Eindruck entsteht, die Statusverteilung wäre Ergebnis individueller Eigenschaften. Wenn dieser „Spagat" gelingt, kann die Übung „Schritt nach Vorn" einen bedeutenden Einfluss auf die Bewusstwerdung von Chancen und Begrenzungen haben, die durch Kategorisierungen entstehen.

Literaturverzeichnis

Bauman, Zygmunt (1992): Moderne und Ambivalenz. Das Ende der Eindeutigkeit. Neuausg., 1. Aufl. Hamburg: Hamburger Ed. Online verfügbar unter http://deposit.dnb.de/cgi-bin/dokserv?id=2631928&prov=M&dok_var=1&dok_ext=htm.

Brander, Patricia (Hg.) (2005): Kompass. Handbuch zur Menschenrechtsbildung für die schulische und außerschulische Bildungsarbeit. Deutsches Institut für Menschenrechte; Bundeszentrale für Politische Bildung. 1. Aufl. Bonn: Bundeszentrale für politische Bildung (Themen und Materialien / Bundeszentrale für politische Bildung). Online verfügbar unter http://kompass.humanrights.ch/cms/front_content.php?idcatart=4.

Hanses, Andreas; Richter, Petra (2011): Die soziale Konstruktion von Krankheit. Analysen biographischer Selbstthematisierungen an Brustkrebs erkrankter Frauen und ihre Relevanz für eine Neubestimmung professioneller Praxis. In: Gertrud Oelerich und Hans-Uwe Otto (Hg.): Empirische Forschung und Soziale Arbeit. Wiesbaden: VS Verlag für Sozialwissenschaften.

Hess, Henner; Scheerer, Sebastian (2014): Theorie der Kriminalität. In: Henning Schmidt-Semisch, Henner Hess und Sebastian Scheerer (Hg.): Die Sinnprovinz der Kriminalität. Zur Dynamik eines sozialen Feldes. Wiesbaden: Springer VS, S. 17–46.

Hirschauer, Stefan (Hg.) (2014): Un/doing differences. Praktiken der Humandifferenzierung. Velbrück GmbH Bücher und Medien. Erste Auflage. Weilerswist: Velbrück Wissenschaft.

Hradil, Stefan (2001): Soziale Ungleichheit in Deutschland. 8. Aufl. Opladen: Leske + Budrich (UTB für Wissenschaft Soziologie, 1809). Online verfügbar unter http://www.socialnet.de/rezensionen/isbn.php?isbn=978-3-8100-3000-9.

Kessler, Suzanne J.; MacKenna, Wendy (1978): Gender. An ethnomethodological approach. New York: Wiley (A Wiley-Interscience Publication).

Kluckhohn, C. (1951): Values and Value-Orientations in the Theory of Action. In: Talcott Parsons und Edward A. Shils (Hg.): Towards a General Theory of Action. New York-Evanstown.

Meuser, Michael (2010): Geschlecht und Männlichkeit. Soziologische Theorie und kulturelle Deutungsmuster. 3. Aufl. Wiesbaden: VS Verl. für Sozialwiss.

Scherr, Albert (2014): Diskriminierung und soziale Ungleichheiten. Erfordernisse und Perspektiven einer ungleichheitsanalytischen Fundierung von Diskriminierungsforschung und Antidiskriminierungsstrategien. Wiesbaden: Imprint: Springer VS (Essentials).

WILDLIFE IN TH SOUTH I

by
Gordon Waterhouse

ORCHARD PUBLICATIONS
2 Orchard Close, Chudleigh, Devon TQ13 0LR
Telephone: (01626) 852714

ISBN 1898964 58 0

Printed by
Hedgerow Print, Crediton, Devon EX17 1ES

Contents

Introduction

Join me exploring the countryside of the South Hams. The walks are between three and eight miles and most are designed to pass by cafés or pubs to provide pleasant comfort stops.

The aim is to guide you through beautiful countryside, pointing out some of the plants and creatures you might see. Even if you do not find all that you hoped to, you are bound to discover other treasures. As you walk, I hope like me, you will be "Surprised by joy," in our South Hams landscape.

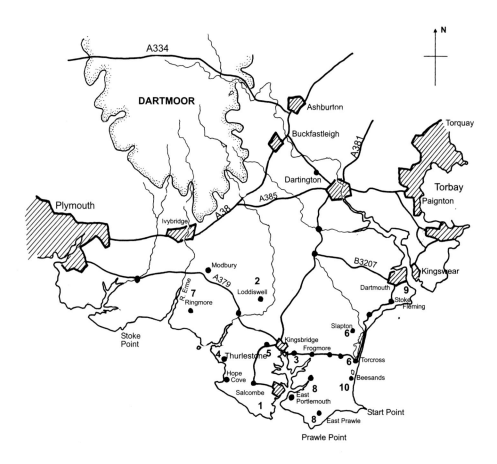

A334

DARTMOOR

Ashburton

Buckfastleigh

A381

Torquay

Dartington

Torbay

Plymouth

A385

Paignton

A38

Ivybridge

B3207

Kingswear

Modbury

A379

2

Dartmouth

9

R. Erme

Loddiswell

Stoke
Fleming

7

Ringmore

Slapton

6

Stoke
Point

Kingsbridge

5

3

Frogmore

4 Thurlestone

6 Torcross

Beesands

Hope
Cove

8

10

Salcombe

East
Portlemouth

Start Point

1

8 East Prawle

Prawle Point

N

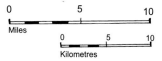

0   5   10
Miles

0   5   10
Kilometres

1. SALCOMBE AND BOLT HEAD

North Sands, Starehole Bay, Bolt Head, Tor Woods, Combe, Collaton and
Hangar Mill
Distance: 7 miles.
Parking at North Sands car park, near the Winking Prawn café.

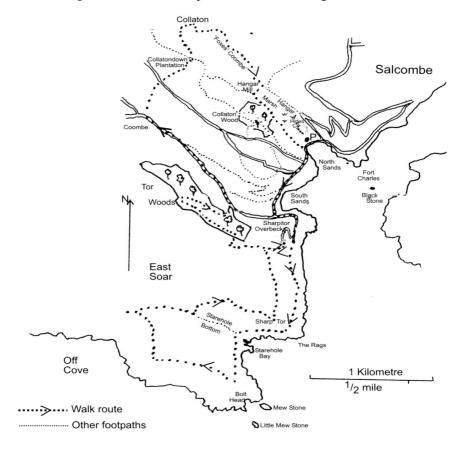

Begin at North Sands car park. Two thousand years ago, a picturesque creek
led inland, between wooded slopes, where North Sands car park now spreads.
The men and women, fishing and cooking by the shore, would have been Iron
Age people, dressed in roughly woven cloth and animal skins. There is evidence
that their ancestors had lived in the South Hams for thousands of years.

The old creek has silted up over the centuries; rushes, reed swamp and
woodland have followed each other. These have been submerged by rising sea
levels and the whole process begun again and again.

There is a board walk which takes you past the latest reed beds, reed-grass and hemlock water-dropwort into the middle of old Hangar Creek. A few towering clumps of tussock sedge grow amongst the reeds. Alder, pussy willow and sycamore trees are already established. From a hide you can look out onto the pond where, in summer, black-tailed skimmers and other dragonflies fly low over the water. Mallard ducks and moorhens shovel and peck in the water. In spring chiffchaffs chip out their repetitive notes from the branches of the pussy willows. In summer reed and sedge warblers sing from the reeds and undergrowth.

The walk continues by taking the lane towards South Sands, round zigzag bends. There is a fine view across the sands to Fort Charles. Growing on the roadside banks are sweet violets, dog's mercury and ramsons, with dark clumps of butcher's broom. As the road comes down to South Sands, holm oaks arch out over the road and the cliffs, framing the view of the sandy cove and its old lifeboat shed.

Across the estuary is the green, conical Wolf Rock buoy and the jagged rocks of the Blackstone. Shags, and their larger relatives the cormorants, perch on the Blackstone, spreading their wings to dry and help digest their last meal. In spring and autumn Sandwich terns dive into the water or rest, with the shags and gulls on the Blackstone. Oystercatchers hunt for limpets to hammer off the rock.

Continue walking along the road following the sign to Overbecks Youth Hostel and Bolt Head. About 100 metres after the wooden kiosk, where the National Trust collect parking fees in summer, there is a fork. Take the left hand track, marked 'Starehole 3/4', not the metalled road, marked Y.H.A. The round leaves of winter heliotrope smother the bank by the fork. Under the trees to your left, naturalised cyclamen are a picture in the autumn. By Bar Lodge cottage, there are glimpses out across the bar. Large numbers of shags, up to a hundred in the autumn, are attracted by the good fishing over the bar. Cormorants sometimes roost in the trees which grow precariously on the steep cliffs below Bar Lodge. The shoals of sand-eels and good visibility in the shallow water, make this a favourite fishing ground for the Sandwich terns, feeding up on their way from their nesting grounds on sand dunes round the North and Baltic seas to the coasts of Angola, where they spend the winter.

The path now goes through woodland; dog's mercury, red campion, ramsons, bluebells, wood avens, wood speedwell and wood sedge are joined by the American invader, pink purslane. In the thickest mounds of bramble, blackcaps nest. Tree creepers, blue tits and great tits search the mossy trunks of the oak trees for insects.

Where the path emerges into the open, is the first climbing corydalis, a weak climber, rather like a cream-flowered fumitory. It is a south-western plant and this walk passes many flourishing patches. On the left is a huge boulder of mica-schist, cloaked with mosses and lichen. One of the lichens - map lichen - is bright green, with a network of thin black lines, like a map. An oak tree hangs over the boulder.

The next part of the walk is through newly sprouting trees and shrubs. Without grazing animals, the grassy cliff-slopes naturally evolve into scrub woodland. Along the grassy path-side, are sea campion, foxgloves, and broom. Bracken shoots up around and above them. To the left is a wonderful view along the coast past Rickham Sands, the white buildings of Gara Rock Hotel, with Prawle Point and its Coast Watch station in the far distance. Ahead is the rugged skyline of The Rags, a saw-like ridge of mica-schist. Ravens often fly overhead, giving their deep, throaty "kronk". The wedge-shaped tail separates them from the crows, rooks or jackdaws. They nest on the rocky outcrops and cliffs, starting in February, constructing or adding to old nests, with twisted branches of gorse and a lining of sheep's wool.

Shortly before you reach The Rags, there is a grassy slope down to the sea and a great rocky stack offshore, zoned with lichens: black like tar, near the tide-line, orange-yellow higher up, especially where birds perch and add their nutrients, and grey on the upper cliffs. The grassy slopes below and above the path are rich in flowers. White stars of English stonecrop, flushed with pink, and pink-purple mats of thyme spread over the bare rock. In Maytime the coastal grassland is speckled with white, yellow and pink — sea campion, kidney vetch and thrift. Later they give way to the yellow-centred ox-eye daisies and the white umbels of wild carrot. Climb up steps to pass through the towering, jagged rocks. Henry Williamson called these rocks 'Valhalla'. There are no Valkyries or eagles here now, but kestrels, peregrine falcons and ravens soar over the highest crags.

Over the safety rail, below The Rags, a beautiful view opens out, across Starehole Bay. This is the last resting place of the Finnish sailing ship, Herzogin Cecilie, wrecked in 1936; its outline can still be seen at very low tides. On the thin soil by the path, is a rock garden of Portland spurge, sheepsbit, madder, bloody cranesbill, carline thistle and the parasitic, ivy broomrape. In June, the sweet-scented, cream flowers of the windpruned privet and the purple-red flowers of bell heather attract butterflies, including the dark green fritillary, whose caterpillars feed on the violet leaves.

The path continues downhill, past thickets of wind-clipped blackthorn, gorse and the smaller western gorse, which has curved spines. Gorse is at its best in April, western gorse in August. Early in the year, celandines, violets, early scurvy grass and climbing corydalis grow by the path. Later, bloody cranesbill, foxgloves, low bushes of bell heather and prickly clumps of butcher's broom take over. In front of the wooden seat, about half way down the sloping path, is a patch of crow garlic. After passing the old ruins, where the cable once started to make the under sea telephone link with America, cross the stream.

In any of the gorse or blackthorn thickets here, you may catch a glimpse of a whitethroat, brown and grey, with a strikingly white chin. They are migrants from Africa and have a churring alarm call and a scratchy song, sometimes given while they fly. The grey and wine-red Dartford warbler has spread along the heathlands of Southern Britain, and sometimes nests in the gorse along our walk. George Montagu of Kingsbridge was the first to describe their nest.

The grassy path branching off to the right, up Starehole valley, makes a short-cut, missing out Bolt Head. For Bolt Head and its spectacular cliff slopes, keep to the sloping path straight on, finger-posted 'Bolt Head'.

At the top of the climb, you can rest on the stone seat and admire the view eastwards along to Prawle Point and down to the Mewstone and the Little Mew Stone, the black islets, encircled by restless surf. Herring gulls, shags and black-backed gulls perch and nest on the Mew Stone. On a sunny day, this is a classic site for butterflies. Graylings rest on the path and bare rock, their mottled grey wings closed and angled to give only the narrowest of shadows. Green hairstreaks flutter around the gorse bushes, keeping to their small territories. Silver-studded, as well as common blue butterflies, take nectar from the flowers that speckle the green sward. First to flower is early scurvy grass, like sprinkled salt in March. Thrift, sea campion and many others follow, with the rusty red patches of sheep's sorrel. The rounded hummocks of summer gorse have been merging to form a solid, prickly mass across the hillside, often with a rosy web of dodder stems. This parasite, which has globules of pink flowers in late summer, has no leaves, because it draws its nourishment from the gorse.

Continue past the old World War II look-out and up a steep, grassy slope. In the shaded crevices of the rocky outcrop, to your left, lanceolate spleenwort grows. It is a Lusitanian plant - one restricted to the western seaboard of Europe.

Near the top of the very steep slope, some chamomile grows among the grass, a natural 'chamomile lawn'. Continue through the wall and turn left to get a view down the cliffs from the rocky pavement.

Follow the winding path near the cliff-top, through gorse scrub and beautiful coastal flowers. Yellowhammers and stonechats may appear on the spikey tops of the gorse and linnets take off with bouncing flight and twittering calls over the scrub, which hides their nests.

When you reach a grassy headland with pearly-white, quartz boulders, you can look down into Off Cove. The winding path turns right along the edge of the cove. When it joins the main cliff path, turn left until you come to a meeting of several paths and a finger post. Take the hairpin turn, right, down to Starehole Bottom. By the stream are clumps of tussock sedge and below, a patch where pimpernel, marsh pennywort, ragged robin and square-stemmed St.John's wort grow. This patch is threatened by encroaching scrub and bracken.

Climb the stile, and cross the stream. Take the Sharp Tor and Overbecks path, up the steps which climb the northern slope of the valley, keeping the farm buildings on your left. Once at the top, there are views down to Starehole Bay and beyond.

On Sharp Tor, a plinth, with a compass diagram, showing distances, such as 'Eddystone 21 miles' and 'Prawle 3 miles' is mounted. To the north you can see Salcombe, the harbour and North Sands, where we began our walk. Continue along this upper cliff path. In gaps cut in the dense blackthorn scrub, glades of foxgloves erupt, their dormant seeds woken by the returning sunlight. There are two, short spur paths off to the right. leading to rocky promontories, where you can look down to the spreading oak woods and Overbecks garden. On the left is a concrete trig. point; a view extends north to Malborough village, the rolling plateau of the South Hams and the blue hills of Dartmoor. Soon after, the path descends some steps, flanked by red campion and shaded by a fine ash tree on the right. At the bottom of the steps, you can make an enjoyable diversion by turning right and following the path for about 200 metres to Overbecks museum and garden, a National Trust property. But our route turns left at the bottom of the steps, towards Tor Woods. Continue along the grassy path and over a stile. Turn right at the next junction, climbing another stile, and enter Tor Woods by a swing gate. The path goes left, along the top of the wood. In spring, primroses and celandines, wood sorrel, wood speedwell, red campion, sorrel and pink purslane grow by the path and bluebells spread under the oak and sycamore trees. There are dark, prickly clumps of butcher's broom. After about a quarter of a mile, the path turns sharply right, by a patch of golden saxifrage and moss-covered logs, and begins to slope downhill. On the old stone walls and gateposts on the left and rocky outcrops on the right of the path are rich growths of moss, including the delicate tamarisc moss, and wall pennywort. In spring the wood is alive with woodland birdsong. At the bottom of the slope the path leads out onto the lane.

Turn left along the attractive lane for half a mile, passing Southern Mill Farm. Shining cranesbill and many other

Sweet violet

hedgerow flowers flourish. Rare cuckoo pint is here, greater

5

periwinkle and lots of sweet violets. The valley bottom is old pasture and the valley slopes are open oak woodland.

Opposite the thatched cottages in the hamlet of Combe, turn right up a steep 'green lane', sunken between honeysuckle-veiled hedge-banks. At the top of the track you can look back across the valley to Tor Woods. When you meet a metalled lane, cross it and climb the stile on the other side. Set out across the open field, in the direction of the finger post, and soon Salcombe appears over the brow of the hill; a glorious view. There is a gate and stile in the gorse hedge ahead. Aim for the stile, climb it and turn left along the hedge, passing a thicket of gorse on your right. Where the hedge meets a line of weather-beaten sweet chestnut trees, is a grassy knoll, ideal for a picnic or a short rest. There is a buzzard's eye view down North Sands valley, with a glimpse of the estuary. Linnets may be twittering in the gorse, the red patches on the males' breasts shining in the sun.

Turn right, beside the line of chestnuts, and sharply left down to two gates and a stile. Take the one on the right, to join a major track. Cross this track. Climb the stile by the gate, which brings you into a field, with a fence on your right. In summer this path is flanked by nettles and thistles and you find the black caterpillars of peacock butterflies or the black and tan ones of small tortoiseshells. At the end of this path, go over a stile and turn right along a lane. After about 100 metres, keep straight on along the footpath and track to Lower Collaton Barn. This track bends right and then a path turns off sharply left. It goes over a wooden bridge, shaded by several horse chestnut trees; the children at Salcombe School call it 'Conker Bridge'.

Turn left, keeping to the path, down a pretty valley, where you may see a fox on his morning patrol. To the left are hazel, oak, ash and sallow and at the bottom, by the stream, some slender alder trees. On the shaded bank to the right of the stream are a host of 'wild' daffodils, which are a picture in March.

Go through the gate ahead, keeping the stone wall, spiked with wall pennywort, on your right. The path climbs up above a bank and another stone wall into a sloping pasture field, ribbed with the ridges of soil creep. Walk along the ridges, to a lone post, which signs the way, until another combe joins the valley from the left. By an old sycamore tree, there is a gate. Go through the gate and listen for the songs of the hedgerow birds. This is where I often hear the rattling song of the cirl bunting, first recorded in Britain by George Montagu. On your right is a steep, bracken-clad slope, on your left a marsh - the top end of Hangar Creek. By mid-summer the marsh is overgrown with chest-high, hemlock water-dropwort, interspersed with patches of sharp-flowered rush, marsh thistle, ragged robin, milk maids - also known as ladies' smock - and clumps of tussock sedge. Where the path curves left and crosses the little stream, look for the metallic blue-green body and folded wings of the beautiful demoiselle damselflies, perched on leaves or fluttering weakly above the stream. Listen to the gentle cadence of the willow warblers, 'as soft as summer rain', singing from the pussy willow bushes in the valley bottom. The spear leaves and flamboyant, yellow blossoms of the flag iris grow here and the first tall stems of common reed and reed-grass. The path goes into the garden of Hangar Mill house. Take the right turn, through a gate, crossing the valley on the bridle path for 100 metres. Where it meets the path along the shady bottom of Collaton Wood, turn left. The dark green leaves of dogs' mercury, a plant of old woodland and ancient hedges, grow beside the path. The insignificant, green flowers are out only from February to April but the leaves remain all through the summer. In April ramsons border the path but by the end of May the flowers and leaves have withered away. Green woodpeckers, as well as the more common great spotted kind, nest in Collaton Wood. Their laughing cry, or yaffle, is as raucous as a kukaburra's. On the sunnier, left-hand side of the path, butterflies, such as red admirals and commas, feast on the blackberry blossom and berries. Robin's pincushion galls often grow on the wild roses climbing the hedge. Dark bush-crickets scrape out their high-pitched songs; the female's curved ovipositor looks like a pirate's scimitar. In October, hundreds of spiders' orb webs are slung from the brambles, pearled by dew on misty mornings and late house martins and swallows may be flying over Hangar Marsh, snapping up midges and flies. We have returned to North Sands, where we began.

2. ANDREW'S WOOD AND BLACKDOWN RINGS, LODDISWELL
Iron Age hillfort and Norman castle, meadows, woodland and Andrew's Wood,
a very special Nature Reserve
Length: 4 miles.
Parking at Blackdown Rings and Andrew's Wood car parks.

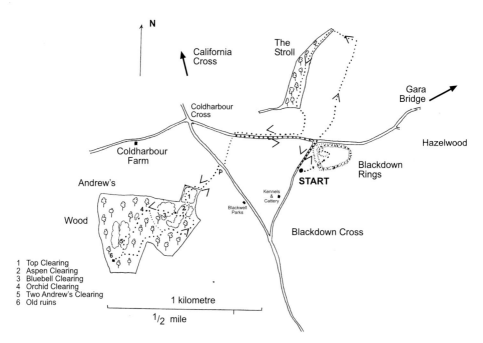

1 Top Clearing
2 Aspen Clearing
3 Bluebell Clearing
4 Orchid Clearing
5 Two Andrew's Clearing
6 Old ruins

1 kilometre

1/2 mile

This is a time-travel walk. Pass through the kissing gate at Blackdown Rings car park to find a huge slab of Staddon grit, veined with quartz. On it is recorded the donation of Blackdown Rings, in 1988, to the Arundel Trust, named after Hatch Arundell, a house connected with Sir Walter Raleigh's family. For many, years Blackdown Rings had been part of the Hazelwood Estate owned by the Peeks. Captain Peek decided to give it to the trust, so that future generations could enjoy this wonderful site.

The circuit of 'The Rings' starts here, by the hawthorn and blackthorn thicket that shelters the picnic tables. In March and April, the blossom of 'blackthorn winter' drifts on the wind like snow. A month later the creamy sprays of May blossom spread along the leafy branches of the hawthorn. Examine the spiny twigs of both and they are smothered with tufted and crusty lichens.

Walk across the pasture land, towards the Iron Age earth works and you may see mole hills, erupting from the green sward. A mole lives his solitary life up here, patrolling the network of tunnels to snatch his daily diet of worms. In mid-winter and early spring he is especially active, clearing out the deeper tunnels, which he hasn't visited since last winter. His brief and violent romance follows. His partner will give birth in her own tunnels, sometime in May, after which her vagina closes completely until next spring and it is back to the celibate life.

At the entrance to the old hill fort is an illustrated information board, showing how it may have looked two thousand years ago, in Iron Age times. Follow the rampart of the fort around to the right and enjoy the wonderful views southwards over the South Hams to the silvery sea of Bigbury Bay. Much closer, the clump of beech trees at Fernhill stands out, just north of Loddiswell. The bank provides a well drained warren for the burrowing rabbits, who have no closed-season for romance. On the bank grow heathy grasses, like sheep's fescue and the little dock, sheep's sorrel, with its small, arrow-shaped leaves. In the autumn it is rich in fungi, such as the yellow, red and white wax-caps, earth balls, sulphur tuft and fairy clubs. Clumps of gorse grow there too, always in flower; 'when kissing's out of season, then gorse is out of bloom' - true for rabbits, if not moles.

From the ditch and embankment grow several mature ash trees; a mass of pinnate leaves, each with nine or eleven leaflets, in summer. They are one of the first trees to lose their leaves in the autumn, showing the beautiful tracery of branches and stout twigs, curving up at the tips, with stubby, black buds. From some, hang the bunches of seeds appropriately called ash keys. There are also rowans, or mountain ashes, which have similar leaves but are unrelated. The grey-barked rowans have frothy, cream blossom in early summer and clusters of orange berries by late summer. Flocks of mistle thrushes come to feast on these and the hawthorn berries.

At the south-east corner of the hill-fort, on the left, is a young sycamore tree; it is our commonest species of maple. In winter its green buds are distinctive.

The oaks, with their gnarled branches, contorted twiggery and cloak of mosses and grey beard-lichens grow mostly along the east and north sides, together with brown birches and rowans.

At the north-west corner of the hill fort are the remains of a mound which the Normans built soon after 1066. On top would have been a wooden stockade castle and around it, a protected area for garrison living quarters - the typical motte and bailey plan of early Norman castles. Climb onto the motte, through the oaks, holly, sallow and rowan bushes, and stand where the Norman sentries stood, with a panoramic view from Salcombe in the south to Dartmoor in the north. To the east is the modern communications mast 'the pylon with plates' at Stanborough, the site of another Iron Age hill fort. A granite plinth has been enscribed with the points of the compass and distant landmarks, such as Start Point and Haytor Rocks.

Returning to the car park, turn right along the lane. On the banks grow polypody fern, bracken, billberry, bell heather, ling and rowan bushes - evidence of the heathland nature of this ridge. On the left, before the road junction, is a fine patch of rose-bay willow-herb - fireweed - a tall plant, which is a blaze of pink-purple in July and August.

At the road junction, take the permissive path signed northwards, through the gate and across the pasture field, keeping the open storage barn on your left. At the foot of the first grassy slope, newly planted with trees, is an old, oakwood copse, to which this new permissive path takes us. The copse is locally called 'The Stroll', a name for a strip of glebeland. The path heads slightly right, downhill towards the junction of two hedges. Where the path passes through the hedge on your left there are hawthorn and hazel; from January to March the hazel bushes are decorated with lambs-tail catkins and tiny, red-spidery, female flowers. Carry on down the slope; the hedge on the right has a lot of holly. The holly leaf-miner fly's grubs live in holly leaves, leaving a pale blotch mark.

At the bottom of the hill, go through the gap in the hedge and turn left, across a grassy field with clumps of soft rush. Head for a gate at the right hand end of the copse. Once through the gate the path goes left, follows a small stream for a few metres and crosses a wire fence by a little stile, into the wood. You are now in The Stroll. Almost immediately on your left is an ancient oak. I call it a belly-button oak, for the old trunk is smothered with the fleshy, belly-button like leaves of wall pennywort and the drooping fronds of polypody ferns. The path meanders through the wood for about quarter of a mile, under the canopy of oaks, while, in April and May the ground is carpeted with bluebells and the cuckoo calls.

From the gate at the end of The Stroll, the path goes uphill, through recently planted woodland. Keep the hedgebank on your left.

At the top of the hill, the path turns right, following the lane hedge. There is another magnificent view to Dartmoor with a recently planted wood in the foreground.

Where the path comes out on to the lane, you can return to Blackdown Rings by turning left back along the lane but our walk continues to Andrew's Wood. Cross the lane and take the footpath, across the fields for a few hundred metres until it comes out on the main road. Cross the road and go through an open gateway into the car park to Andrew's Wood, a Devon Wildlife Trust nature reserve.

The history of Andrew's Wood probably goes back three thousand years. The old hedge banks we cross as we walk round

Lobelia

10

the wood may have been part of a pattern of Bronze Age boundaries, the reeve system, which is still visible up on Dartmoor. From Saxon times the area was known as Stanton Moor. In the south-west corner of the reserve are the ruins of a mediaeval farmstead, that Andrew Walker found, when wandering around the wood in his teenage years. By careful clearance, Andrew revealed beneath the pile of stone rubble, the walls, a hearth, bread-ovens and a flight of stone steps. Tragically, in 1969, Andrew was killed in a car accident; he was only in his early twenties.

His parents owned Woolston House and the surrounding farmland, including Stanton Moor. They leased and later sold Stanton Moor to the Devon Wildlife Trust, on one condition, that the name be changed to Andrew's Wood, in memory of their son.

The Devon Trust value it for the rich wildlife in the heathland pasture and woodland and in particular for a rare plant, heath lobelia. Heath lobelia can only germinate in open clearings so, for over thirty years, we have kept these clearings open by cutting, burning and grazing. The beautiful blue-purple spikes of heath lobelia, which Captain Harris Wyse of Woolston House first recorded here on 15th August 1898, grow in only five other sites in Britain. Since 1975 the friends of Andrew's Wood have counted it every year and by management the population has increased from a few hundred plants to over 12,000.

Walk down the track from the car park. Through the first gate is a brown birch, planted in memory of George Watkins, a wonderful naturalist who visited the wood from the 1930s until his death in 1991. The track leads down to the first clearing, Top Clearing, with lovely views across rolling hills to the sea.

Top Clearing is thick with sharp-flowered rush. Enter the clearing by the gate and take the winding path down through the rushy meadow. Two interesting, semi-parasitic plants grow in the shorter grass below the gate - yellow rattle and yellow bartsia. Both have increased since grazing began in the 1990s.

In May, among the rushes, there are pink dapplings of ragged robin, purple spikes of marsh orchids and the bright yellow of lesser spearwort - the buttercup of the moors. Creeping along the ground are bog pimpernel, marsh pennywort and clumps of lesser skullcap. Growing taller than the rushes are marsh thistles and, later in the summer, the smokey-pink heads of hemp agrimony and patches of grey-leaved fleabane with its bright yellow daisy flowers. Butterflies love these plants and love the clearings of Andrew's Wood. First to appear are the brimstones, peacocks and tortoiseshells coaxed out of hibernation by the warmth of a sunny day in February or March. Orange-tips, green-veined whites and holly blues join them in April and later the skippers, the whites, the common blue, commas, painted ladies, red admirals and perhaps clouded yellow. By August the big, orange, silver-washed fritillaries are gliding along the clearings and resting on the bramble blossom. It is here in Top Clearing that you will see your first heath lobelia, in flower from late June till October.

Look out for the engraved wooden posts, to follow the Frog Trail (about half a mile) or the Beetle Trail (about a mile). Once through the gate at the bottom of Top Clearing, stop, stand and admire the next clearing - Aspen Clearing. A buzzard may take off from the glade of tall aspens down on the left. On a quiet day listen for the rustling of the aspen leaves, like the rippling of a stream.In early summer you will hear the silvery, five second cadence of the willow warblers; migrants from Africa, they nest in the tussocky grass.

Turn right, through the kissing gate, and you will come to a little pool, near the storage hut. Frogspawn may be laid here in January. In this little clearing you will usually hear the rich song of a blackcap in April and May, his brown-capped mate will be sitting on a nest, hidden in the brambles nearby.

Walk on and you enter Bluebell Clearing. Once it was cultivated, for on the tithe map of 1839 it is called Oat Moor. Now it is carpeted with bluebells and, as the blue carpet withers, up shoots a forest of bracken. Violets thrive in this drier clearing and pearl bordered fritillaries used to flutter along the path feeding on the nectar of bugle flowers and searching for violets on which to lay their eggs. Two big bushes of guelder rose, at least fifty years old, grow in the middle of Bluebell Clearing; in summer they are decorated by creamy-white hemispheres of blossom, in autumn by clusters of red berries. Around the clearing, birds sing from the thick scrub of hazel, blackthorn and birch. Beneath the scrub is hidden a fox's earth. At dusk, I have seen a family of fox cubs playing among the bluebells.

Pass through the next gate, walk under ancient hedgerow oaks and onto a sturdy board-walk. In February and March, golden saxifrage spreads, green-gold, beside the walkway. The path has been widened, so that the Trust can take cattle or ponies to graze in the Two Andrews' clearing further on in the reserve.

Against some of the trees you will see nest-boxes. In May, you might see a blue, great, coal or marsh tit, or a nuthatch, bringing a beakful of green caterpillars to its hungry chicks. Dormice also use the boxes but remember it is illegal to disturb dormice, without a special licence. Please do not open the boxes.

The path bears left and passes a small clearing on your right, where heath spotted orchids grow among tussocky purple moor-grass, hence its name of Orchid Clearing. Small amounts of all three common species of heather grow here - bell heather, ling and cross-leaved heath - and tussocks of purple moor-grass and tufted hair-grass, one of our tallest and most spectacular grasses.

Leaving Orchid Clearing, the path comes to an old hedgebank Mossy Bank - and a deeply entrenched stream. Most of the old banks in the reserve have a fine selection of mosses, liverworts and ferns, including the south-western speciality, hay-scented buckler fern, but this bank is exceptional. The recently widened Trolls' Bridges take us over two streams; take a look down, in case the troll is lurking underneath, and admire the variety of these primitive but beautiful non-flowering plants. Then pause to look for birds in the canopy above.

Soon we enter the last big clearing. By the mid-1970s, the western part of this clearing, where sneezewort and lobelia once grew, had been swallowed up by encroaching pussy-willow and birch. Despite regular clearance, by 2000 it looked as if the whole clearing would become woodland; five years without major clearance and it was head high in scrub. Now it has been cleared and fenced so that it can be grazed. This is the Two Andrews' clearing, in memory of Andrew Walker and Andrew Shaw, both of whom were killed in road accidents. During an earlier clearance, about twenty years ago, many seedling oaks were cut down or removed for replanting but two were left - a memorial to the Two Andrews. The trees have a good lichen flora developing on the ribbed trunks and hanging from the branches. In July and August, you can sometimes see purple hairstreak butterflies fluttering around the tops of the Andrews' oaks.

Lobelia grows here and two other purple-blue flowers - saw-wort and devilsbit scabious. The scabious, which flowers in the autumn, is the food plant for the marsh fritillary butterfly, which used to occur in Andrew's Wood. Several alder buckthorn bushes, their twigs almost black, are left on purpose, as the leaves are the food for brimstone butterfly caterpillars. Near the top of the clearing is a colony of over fifty twablade orchids. Along the northern and western ditches are regal stands of royal fern and we hope to recreate a pond in the very wet area of sphagnum and bog pondweed, where bogbean used to grow.

The path goes down the clearing and into the wood to a T junction. Turn right and in a few hundred metres, having ducked beneath a giant oak (toppled in the hurricane of 1989) and weaved left and right over the old field boundaries, you find the ruins where we tread on the dreams of many generations, these ruins, which Andrew excavated, were home to farming families from mediaeval to Victorian times. The thatched roof has fallen in and rotted away but Andrew uncovered the walls, bread ovens and a flight of steps. We felled a tree growing from one of the old walls and counted over a hundred tree-rings. Monkshood, star of Bethlehem and gooseberry bushes still grow in the walled space that was their garden.

Retrace your steps to the T junction and continue straight on, completing the circuit of the Beetle Trail, twisting and turning along bilberry-covered banks and through ferny woodland. It is here on the damp ferny floor of the wood, that you may disturb a woodcock, rising silently on bowed, bracken-brown wings, through the birch trees. All the birch trees in Andrew's Wood are brown birches but they still have beautiful silvery trunks. Some of these are nearing the end of their life-span of about seventy years. Birch trees grow twiggy galls - witches' brooms - which can be mistaken for birds nests hanging in the delicate twiggery. In their old age they are prey to a bracket fungus, the birch polypore, which softens the tissue of the heart wood. Great spotted woodpeckers can then excavate their nests in the old birches; you may hear their drumming, echoing on a spring morning.

Another ten minutes walking and you find yourself back in Aspen Clearing, having made a circuit of Andrew's Wood. Retrace your steps up to the car park and along to Blackdown and its fabulous view, where you began.

3. FROGMORE to WEST CHARLETON
Creekside, marsh, combe and lane
Length: 5 miles.
Parking: There is parking over the creek-head bridge in Frogmore.

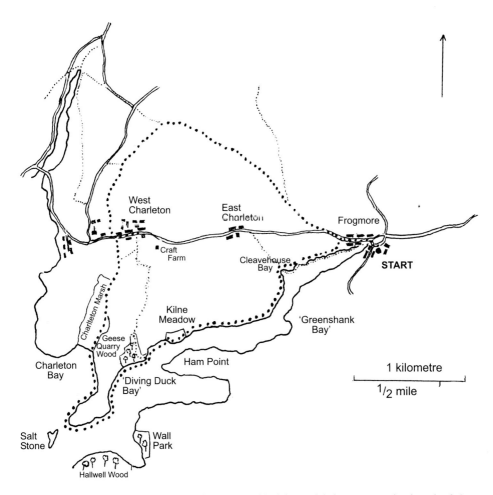

Opposite Frogmore Bakery is the road bridge which crosses the head of the creek and leads to South Pool and Prawle. From the bridge you can watch the stream coming into the muddy estuary. The latest brood of swans often gather here, an egret or two, a flock of black-headed gulls, some redshank and perhaps a greenshank.

From the bridge, walk up the main road. A public footpath takes you along the northern shore of Frogmore Creek to Cleavehouse Bay. The footpath is signposted about 200 metres above the Globe Inn on the left hand side of the main road. The path skirts a pasture field and follows the hedge by the low cliff above the estuary. The 'warden of the estuary', the redshank, may yelp a warning and fly off, showing white trailing edges to the wings. In the curve of the creek may be more redshanks and sometimes a flock of about a dozen egrets. At Cleavehouse Bay, there is an attractive, little salt-marsh with sea plantain and sea arrow-grass, lilac-pink stars of sea spurrey and later, tall, mauve-rayed sea asters.

Past the bay, through the netted branches of the blackthorn and hawthorn hedge, are glimpses of the creek. Across on the far side is 'greenshank bay', a favourite gathering place for these elegant, grey and white waders. In September, there may be about twenty of them along 'greenshank bay'.

Recently, through the Countryside Stewardship scheme, farmers have left uncultivated margins between the estuary and the fields. This saves tons of silt and fertilizer run-off being washed into the estuary and provides an important habitat for plants, insects and birds. Arable weeds, no longer common, grow at the edge of the crop: field madder, field woundwort, corn spurrey, fluellen and scarlet pimpernel. In the hedgerow and in the fields beside them, may be flocks of linnets, greenfinches and charms of goldfinches. Skylarks feed in the stubble fields in winter, flying up with a rippling flight, their call a liquid trill. Finches and larks have increased since fields of stubble have been left through the winter - providing them with food.

Soon, the footpath slips through a hedgebank and we are in a meadow of rough grassland - Kilne Meadow. This meadow was purchased in 1931 by Mr.Young, son of the Rector of Charleton, for his family to come camping on their holidays. They erected sheds to serve as accommodation. They planted shrubs and everlasting sweet peas and put up a garden swing - all of which are still there today. For twenty years it provided a magical place for the family. Tessa Young remembers these holidays so well and recalls them in her reminiscences - 'Shangri-la on Frogmore Creek'. She and her brother would row across to Ham Point, which they called 'Our Island' and set nets across the creek at night, to catch mullet and mackerel, like a Swallows and Amazons family. Their mother would cook the mackerel in oats for breakfast. Fifty years on, butterflies and bush crickets bask in the summer sun, voles thrive in the long grass and kestrel, buzzard and perhaps a barn owl hunt over this little paradise. The fish are still there in the creek and the herons and occasional osprey still enjoy them.

The footpath leaves Kilne Meadow and goes down by a stream to follow the foreshore. The rocky foreshore is slippery, so go carefully. Channel and spiral wracks, the weeds that grow highest on the shore, and knotted wrack and saw wrack, which grow lower down, cover the rocks in a twisted, slimy forest.

Ahead is Geese Quarry Wood. The walk continues westwards past the wood, along the shore. This section is the best for birdwatching but do not attempt it within two hours of high tide. There is a short-cut path which leads up through Geese Quarry Wood and over the fields to Charleton. The foreshore consists of flat, slatey fragments; slate was quarried at Geese Quarry for centuries.

Across the creek at Ham Point, oystercatchers and curlew often gather at high tide. I call the wide bay that opens up to the right, 'diving duck bay', for this is the best place to see goldeneye, red-breasted mergansers and other diving duck in the winter. Great crested and little grebes also fish here. Across this bay stretches North Pool Bay, an undisturbed sanctuary for waders and flocks of wigeon in the winter. At low tide there is an expanse of rich mud, at high tide a broad lake.

Carry on along the tide line, around 'diving duck bay' to the spit of shingle, where cormorants and oystercatchers sometimes perch at high tide. The oaks around the bay are so sheltered from the westerly winds they stretch out luxuriantly over the beach and are some of the first to come into leaf. The Rogers family, who farm here, and the estuary Conservation Officer, Nigel Mortimer, have helped local children plant oak trees around Wareham Point. From the shingle spit, are good views across to Wall Park Plantation, where a few pairs of herons nest, and Halwell Wood.

The cliffs near Wareham Point are of soft fragments called head, brought down in mud-slides during the thawing at the end of the last ice age. Stinking iris, sea-beet and sea spurrey thrive there and rabbits, badgers and foxes burrow in the cliffs.

From Wareham Point you look down to the moored yachts, towards Salcombe and, closer, to the dark islet offshore. This islet is called The Saltstone. George Montagu, one of the fathers of the study of natural history, made many of his discoveries,

Channel, spiral, knotted and saw wracks

of worms, sponges, sea-slugs and crustacea in the early nineteenth century, here. The Saltstone is a protected area and we are requested not to walk out to it.

At migration time waders often stop to rest near Wareham Point and Sandwich terns dive for sand-eels off the Saltstone. As the tide floods, this islet becomes a roosting site for cormorants and gulls; the greatest number of cormorants are in October, when the residents are joined by young birds from as far as Wales. The record count, of over a hundred, coincided with an amazing influx of sprats and mackerel in the autumn of 2001.

In winter, Wareham Point is a splendid vantage point from which to survey the whole estuary. Black-necked or Slavonian grebes are sometimes seen with the more common great crested and little grebes. It is also the most likely spot to find that wonderful bird, the great northern diver.

Out on Charleton Bay, are shelduck and curlew, a few egrets stalking for little fish in the pools and a heron waiting for unwary eels, flounders or mullet by the muddy channel. In winter they are joined by a flock of brent geese. As you walk along the shore you notice the trees on this exposed, cliff-top are wind pruned, as if the wind was blowing them sideways. A few hundred metres from Wareham Point are several contorted old pear trees, clinging onto the cliff. Along the shore are the ruts of an old cart track, where horses came collecting shellfish and seaweed before the Second World War.

In winter, as the tide rises, wigeon and teal drift up the channel towards the head of the bay, where the sluice discharges from the sea-wall. This sea-wall was built in 1805 to reclaim the creek, which continued inland to Charleton village. Now, there are plans to create a hide on the sea-wall. From here, we will be able to see the muddy bay slowly covered with water and watch the birds being pushed ever closer by the tide. On the other side of the wall we will see West Charleton Marsh. This marsh is a delightful mixture of grassland for the grazing cattle, shallow pools and expanses of reed and sea club-rush.

A pair of kingfishers fish the ditches. Summer visitors to the marsh include reed warblers nesting in the tall reeds, and a few pairs of chattering sedge warblers, which nest in the scrub and thick foliage at the edge of the marsh. A pair of lesser whitethroats often breed in the hedgerows along the old cliff-line by the marsh and sometimes cirl buntings.

In the winter, there are snipe at the edge of the reed beds and around the floodwater pools, and an occasional jack snipe. Wigeon, teal and shelduck, with occasional parties of pintail or shoveler throng these pools on winter mornings. Flocks of curlew and lapwing may roost beside them. The sight of them in flight, weaving patterns against a winter sky, the whistling calls of the wigeon and the bubbling cries of curlew are hauntingly beautiful. Follow the path along the right hand side of the marsh through the wooden gate onto a track under the hedges, which ends at Beverley Curl's lovely artistic recreation of the wildlife to be seen on the marsh. Soon after is the sewage works. Many birds, including wintering chiffchaffs, come to feed on the circular filterbed.

The track leads up from the sewage works to the main road. Carefully cross straight over the road to the public footpath. On the roadside verge, at the start of the footpath, rare cuckoo pint grows. As you walk along the path, very soon you can look back over a garden wall to view the marsh and the open estuary beyond. The path continues, past houses and gardens and up a grassy valley; just the place for a barn owl to drift across the tussocky growth, looking for voles.

Eventually, at a T junction, the path meets a wide, tree fringed track. This was the main mediaeval road from Kingsbridge to Stokenham. Turn right along it. Hedgerow growth obscures the view but it is a sheltered paradise for butterflies. The speckled wood, that prefers the dappled shade among the brambles and hedgerow plants, the peacock and the small tortoise-shell all fly throughout the summer. In April orange-tip and green-veined whites emerge. In July and August, the gatekeeper is abundant, and through into the late autumn the red admirals are usually the most common species.

After about half a mile, there is a gap in the hedge and a fine view of the estuary. Soon afterwards the track turns right, sloping steeply down and becoming a sunken, shaded lane. In wet conditions, you need to take care, for the bedrock - 400 million year old Meadfoot Slate - is very slippery underfoot. Either side of you on the shaded banks hartstongue fern and soft shield fern are abundant. This tunnel of green gloom brings you back to Frogmore.

4. THURLESTONE - BANTHAM

Four streams and a river, sandy beaches and dramatic rocky coast

Length: 5 miles.

Parking at Thurlestone Golf Club, higher car park, Links Court cliff-top car park, Thurlestone Sands National Trust car park or Bantham car park.

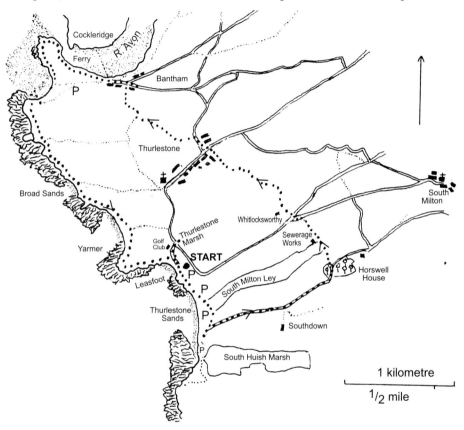

This walk uses both the coastal footpath and inland paths, crossing the valleys of four streams. Start from the car park at Thurlestone Golf Club; pay your fee at the club house.

Walk down, in front of the club-house, to the sea. In early spring, the short turf and wall-tops are speckled lilac-white with the tiny flowers of early scurvy-grass. Leasfoot Beach is a lovely bathing spot in summer, backed by sand dunes, from which thick tussocks of marram-grass sprout, sand sedge spreads out by straight runners and through them both clamber the stems of sea bindweed, with glossy, kidney-shaped leaves and pink trumpet flowers. By the cul-de-sac road behind the beach, the grass is dotted with the pink pompom flowers of thrift and

20

splashed with pale yellow patches of kidney vetch. Later come the darker yellow flowers of eggs and bacon - birdsfoot trefoil - and the yellow speckle-clouds of ladies bedstraw. In high summer the tall purple heads of greater knapweed attract many insects, including the black and red, six-spot burnet moths, and a flourishing patch of sea holly is smothered in smokey-blue flowers, buzzing with bumble bees.

The road narrows to a path by Links Court, where sea beet and pellitory of the wall grow from the dry-stone walls. On the cliff-top is a forest of black mustard, some over two metres high, with clustered heads of yellow flowers in early summer. The pink heads and grassy leaves of rosy garlic sprout among the grasses.

On the cliff-top are stout tree mallows, with velvet-soft leaves and mauve-pink flowers. Stonechats often balance on top of the mallows, flicking their wings and tails and making their 'chack chack' calls.

The path continues across the Links Court car park, to the marram-covered dunes and wooden footbridge that leads across South Milton Ley. The stream curves round the sand dunes, to disappear into a bank of sand or, more often, cutting an impressive, sandy canyon to the sea. Upstream is the great reed-bed, a Devon Bird-watching and Preservation Society reserve and home to the churring reed warblers in summer and the longbilled snipe in winter. A migrating marsh harrier is sometimes seen, flying low over the reeds, in spring or autumn.

Sea Holly and Sea Bindweed

After a few hundred metres you arrive at the snack-bar and public toilets, by the National Trust car park. This area is a regular haunt for black redstarts in late autumn. Out on the wave-cut rocky platform, covered with knotted wrack and other seaweeds, stands Thurlestone Rock, an isolated stack of New Red Sandstone, used as a perch by cormorants in even the strongest gale. At high tide, it is a fine challenge to swim out to the rock from the sandy beach. With a snorkel and mask you can see the weeds waving gently beneath you and shoals of sand-eels swimming through them. At low tide it is a delight for rockpooling.

Standing by the snack-bar, you can view South Huish Marsh, another Devon Bird-watching Society reserve. There are flocks of gulls, perhaps a hundred Canada geese, oystercatchers and sometimes other waders around the edge of the pools. Shoveler duck, the drakes with white breasts and chestnut bellies, gather here, with big flocks of wigeon and teal in the winter. Closer at hand, stonechats, migrating wheatears and whinchats may perch on the posts and barbed wire fence, which forms the boundary of the reserve. In May 2002, four black-winged stilts visited, feeding and displaying around the shallow pools.

Take the lane inland from the snack-bar. Like most of the lanes leading down to the coast, between Hope Cove and Bantham, there is a luxuriant growth of towering black mustard in summer. Alexanders - the umbellifer with yellow-green flowerheads and cloying scent that grows especially near the sea - is dominant in spring. Stop by the gate on the left, about 300 metres up the lane, for the view over the reed-bed to the sea. A thick mat of old man's beard grows up over the bank.

Just before South Down Farm, on your right, you can glimpse the stubby tower of the ruined church at South Huish, at the head of the valley. After the farm, the hedge on the right of the lane is elm. On the left, roses are abundant, showing their pink and white petals in summer and many robin's pincushion galls in the autumn. On the right, there are clumps of hemp agrimony; especially attractive to red admiral butterflies in late summer.

The lane enters a sycamore plantation, part of the grounds of Horswell House. Encouraged by the shade, the glossy green straps of hartstongue fern and shuttlecocks of soft shield-fern become prolific on the hedge-banks. A fine beech tree overhangs the lane.

Where the wood ends, opposite some old drinking troughs encrusted by liverworts, turn left down the footpath to the top of the great reed-bed of South Milton Ley. The ruins of the old thatcher's cottage stand on the far side. The path crosses the marsh. In summer, among the thick growth of reed-mace, great willow-herb and hemlock water-dropwort, sedge warblers sing their chattering song. In winter water rails skulk along the ditches and make unearthly squeals. Reed buntings, less common than twenty years ago, sometimes perch in the pussy willow bushes.

The path continues past the sewerage works, by a line of elms and hedgerow flowers into the works lane. When you reach the public road, turn left for about a hundred metres and then turn right, between two turkey oaks, down the track to Whitlocksworthy Farm. By the farm buildings, house sparrows may be perched, attracted by spilt grain. Where the track bends sharply left, take the footpath off to the right. Yellow arrows help you follow the path, zig-zagging down to the stream in the bottom of the valley. Cross the stream by an old iron kissing-gate. A mass of fools' watercress - similar to the edible kind but this one is poisonous - grows in the stream, with pussy willows overhead.

The path now follows the edge of a field. Keep the hedge on your right. Turn right over a stile and head up towards the top left corner of the old pasture field.

Thurlestone from Thurlestone Sands

There are patches of spear and creeping thistles; butterflies visit the purple flowers and charms of goldfinches come to feed on the thistledown seeds. Rabbits scuttle away to their warren in the hedgebank. Pied wagtails peck for insects in the pasture and fly away with a 'chizz-ik' call, their long tails trailing behind them.

There is a stile at the top of the field, which leads into a road. Turn left along it and take the second turning on your right, which is signed Public Footpath. This brings you out onto Thurlestone's main road. Turn left, past the school and then right, where there is a sign 'Slow - School Footpath'; this joins the West Buckland lane. Turn right along the lane for about 200 metres and take the footpath on the left, signed 'Bantham 3/4 mile', which follows an old stone wall.

There is a wonderful view; to the right is West Buckland village and ahead Bantham, the mouth of the Avon estuary and Burgh Island. At the end of the wall, the path goes through a gateway into the next field and veers to the right to follow a strip of woodland; a mixture of larch, Scots pine, sycamore, ash and sweet chestnut, together with a few Douglas firs, suffering from old age and salt winds. Under the trees bluebells spread. In winter, the path beside the wood and down by the stream can be very muddy.

At the four-arrow post, at the end of the wood, turn right and over a stile, above the rectangular pond, to cross the stream. A song thrush sometimes uses the block of granite, by the stile, as an anvil to smash snail shells.

23

Turn left, parallel to the stream, and look at the fine nodding thistles which are usually allowed to thrive in the sloping field to your right. By the line of decrepit Monterey pines, turn right, over a stile and up the path, by a clump of bamboo and arching blackthorn hedge. This will bring you to the main street in Bantham, by the Sloop Inn. As you return down past the Sloop, notice the rich flora growing from the walls. Red valerian is a feature of our South Hams walls and it comes in shades of red, pink and white.

Walk on by the car park attendant's hut and take the tarmac track, slightly to the right, from which you have a panoramic view of the lower reaches of the River Avon. By the river, oystercatchers and gulls, herring, lesser and greater black-backs and black-headed gulls gather. A few little egrets prance through the shallows and a heron stands, still as a post. Twenty or more swans often float by on the tide.

In the grass by the path the pink blooms of pyramidal orchid sprout among many other flowers. Bracken is spreading and threatens to overwhelm this rich grassland. Meadow brown, gatekeeper, marbled white and common blue are all common butterflies here.

Just before the little house on your right, the first patch of stinking iris grows on the left of the path. This plant flourishes in the old sand dunes amongst the marram grass. You can follow the path round to the right, keeping to the cliff edge, above the thatched boat-house. The narrow-leaved everlasting pea - a south-western speciality - grows up among the privet bushes on the left of the path. At the mouth of the estuary, you can view the surf, rushing in over the ribbed sands.

Follow the cliff-top path until you come to a flight of steps down onto the beach. Walk across the sands towards the lifesaving look-out. To your left are the sand dunes, held by the deep, spreading roots of the marram grass which has colonised the sandy slopes.

Walk up beside the look-out to join the cliff-path. As the path climbs, pause, to enjoy the view of Bigbury Bay, opening up behind you. Listen for the 'kronk' call of a raven, flying overhead or performing acrobatics in the updraught along the cliff-line. They begin repairing their cliff ledge nests of twisted gorse stems and sheep's wool lining, in January and February. Look down to the shags perched on the Long Stone, a slender stack. A couple of great black-backed gulls often choose to sit, kings of the castle, on top of the offshore rocks.

Thrift, sea campion, kidney vetch and wild carrot create a cliff-top garden beyond which beautiful views open out, across the ever-changing sea, southwards to Hope Cove and the promontory of Bolt Tail and westwards to the misty blue fingers of Cornwall. When you reach a green, corrugated-iron shed there are benches for you to rest. You may see a hovering kestrel, above the coarser grass, searching for voles. Streaking past the cliffs, a peregrine may dive after a flock of jackdaws or an unsuspecting feral pigeon. From January until early autumn, fulmars often patrol this stretch of coast, gliding on straight wings.

Just after the green hut there is a steep path down to Broadsands beach. When there are no people on the beach, oystercatchers often gather there, probing for side-shrimps in the sand. In summer it is a pleasant bathing beach, with good rock-pooling at low tide.

Back up on the cliff-top, continue along the coastal path. On the left is the golf course, which dates back to 1897. Stonechats keep watch over the greens, perched on dock or thistle stalks. To the right and straight ahead are glorious views along the coast. It is worth going down to the next beach, Yarmer, through the fringe of marram-grass and sand dune. Especially after south-westerly gales, many interesting finds have been made along this and other Thurlestone beaches. It may be cargo washed overboard or natural flotsam. Cuttlefish 'bones' and 'mermaids' purses' in which young rays were nurtured, are local relics, from the English Channel. From across the Atlantic come transparent oval disks, the skeletons of by-the-wind sailors and 'goose' barnacles attached to floating timbers. There have been many stranded dolphins and in 2002, a pigmy sperm whale. The path follows on around one more headland to reach Leasfoot Beach. Behind Leasfoot beach is the golf club and the car park - our starting point.

5. KINGSBRIDGE and WEST ALVINGTON

Including Collapit Creek and West Alvington Wood.

Length: 7 miles.

Park in the main car park at the top of Fore Street, near St.Edmund's church - the church with the spire.

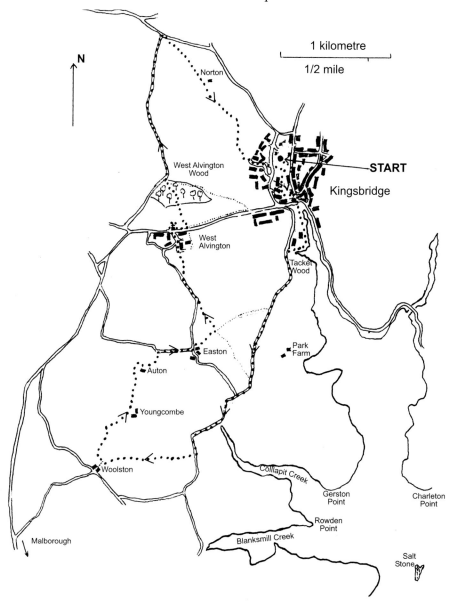

Start by the steps, at the southern end of the car park, which lead up to the back of St. Edmund's Church. A path takes you left to the main street, Fore Street, by the northern door of the church. Above the door is written 'Adeste Fideles' - 'O, Come All ye Faithful'. Turn right, down Fore Street, under the pillars of the old shambles, until, opposite Lloyd's Bank, you turn right down White Hart Passage. This narrow way leads to a mill stream, with a spreading mat of mind-your-own-business growing on the wall above the stream. Eventually the passage curves round to the left and comes out at the bottom of Fore Street. Turn down right and cross to the Tourist Information Centre. At the waterside, by the public conveniences, is a board explaining some of the interesting facts about the changing face of Kingsbridge. London plane trees have been planted in the square in front of the bandstand and, by the quayside, a splendid tree cotoneaster, which was host to a flock of waxwings for one day in 1996.

Walk along the quayside, with the car park on your right. At high tide mallard are joined by swans, reaching up their necks for tit-bits. As the tide goes out, an egret will soon be taking up his fishing station, near where the mill stream comes out, at the head of the quay. Crowds of gulls, mostly black-headed, with some of the bigger, herring gulls, gather. A few redshanks follow the water's edge, with business-like forays across the mud, on quick-moving orange-red legs, probing for rag-worms. As you come near the end of the car park, you may also see a greenshank

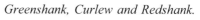

Greenshank, Curlew and Redshank.

or two, paler than the redshank and with grey-green legs. Kingfishers often perch on the gunwales of the dinghies, fishing in the shallow water. Outside the Quayside sports centre, there is a thriving rookery in the tall trees; they start rebuilding their nests in February and by April the young are already hatched. From the slipway at the end of the car park, you can look across to Tacket Wood. This is where George Montagu first saw cirl buntings, which had never before been recorded in Britain; he caught some and kept them in an aviary in his garden, at the top of Fore Street.

Turn right by a footpath sign and follow the path around Tacket Wood creek. Grey squirrels leap through the old oak trees, overhanging the creek, and looking

27

for food in the grounds of the Gordon Carling and Ropewalk Centre. The workers and residents here have a reputation for caring for wildlife and have led the community in recycling projects.

You come to the road, where the creek emerges under a little bridge. Turn right over the bridge and follow the lane up the steep hill. On the shaded banks, as you climb the hill, harts tongue fern is common and a delicate grass, wood melick. Near the top of the hill, on the right, grows bastard-balm, an uncommon plant; a member of the dead-nettle family, found mostly in the south-west.

To your left are striking views across the Kingsbridge Estuary to Charleton Point, the Saltstone and Halwell Wood.

Walk on, the hedgebanks are full of flowers. Plants including lesser celandine, primrose, Alexanders, cow parsley, jack-by-the-hedge, goosegrass, red campion, greater stitchwort, crosswort, bluebell, sorrel, herb robert, foxglove, hogweed, wood sage, hedge bedstraw, mullein and hemp agrimony make a kaleidoscope of changing colour through the year. Our Devon lanes are beautiful, linear nature reserves.

Through the next gate on your left is a view over the estuary to a disused stone quay, jutting out from near High House Point. This is Southville Quay at which the paddle steamer ferries used to call. On your right is a stile and footpath, by which you can take the short-cut route, across the fields to Easton Cross.

By the stile and along the roadside for the next few yards are a wonderful collection of wild geraniums. Round-leaved, shining, Pyrenean, long-stalked, cut-leaved and dovesfoot cranesbills all grow within twenty metres together with the commonest, herb Robert. All have pink or mauve flowers with five petals, although some are divided so it looks as if they have ten.

Follow the road as it bears sharply to the right. Do not take the private South-West Water road which goes straight on.

Ignore the turning to Easton and continue downhill to the bridge over Collapit Creek. From the bridge you look down the narrow, muddy creek, fringed with trees, where egrets sometimes perch. A kingfisher visits regularly and a redshank or greenshank may be walking along the water's edge. Rock samphire grows from the bridge. Below it is an attractive salt-marsh, with sea-asters spearing up from the sward of salt-marsh grass. There are clumps of saltmarsh-sedge and a small meadow of waving sea club-rush, where the short-winged coneheads, a salt-marsh species of bush cricket, leap in mid-summer.

Carry on up the lane, past Rowden Cottage. On the wall beside the cottage, pellitory of the wall and wall pennywort flourish and on top is a fine growth of yellow stonecrop. The round leaves of winter heliotrope grow on the left of the road and dog roses arch up from the hedge on the right.

The lane soon turns sharply to the left and climbs steeply, between bluebell and bracken-covered banks. At the top of the hill, turn right over the gate. There is a public footpath which follows the hedgebank on your right. Look back for a fine view of the serpentine course of Collapit Creek. In the winter you can see flocks of wigeon and teal dabbling in the central channel of the creek.

In summertime, along the hedge to your right, you hear the harsh, chattering song of the whitethroat, the 'nettle-creeper'and the yellowhammer's song of a 'little-bit-of-bread-and-no-cheese'. 'Golden laddies' is their local name. Both are common in the hedges across the higher, arable fields of the South Hams.

Go over the next stile, where you may find common mallow and, our local speciality, balm-leaved figwort growing. On the skyline to the left is upper Salcombe and ahead, the spire of Malborough church. Out over the open fields, in spring, skylarks will be singing. Looking back you can see the whole width of the estuary, up Frogmore Creek, with Halwell Wood at its mouth and Beacon Plantation against the sky.

The footpath eventually becomes a green lane and, just before Woolston, there is a footpath sign to your right, opposite some old man's beard. You are faced with two gates; take the left hand one into a narrow meadow. An old gate post stands in the middle of the meadow, left for the cattle as a scratching post.

If you get confused down the next section, the West Alvington TV mast, standing high on the hill to the north, is a useful land mark to aim for. Start by keeping the hedge on your right, and walk on until you come to a gate on your right. Go through this gate and cross the next field diagonally to the gate in the north-east corner. Go downhill for about 100 metres, turn left at the corner and through the next gate on your left. Head diagonally right, where a gate leads into the farm road at Youngcombe Farm.

Please shut the gate after you and keep the farm buildings on your right. The track passes an open barn and heads for the TV mast. This valley, with its small, hedged fields is good cirl bunting habitat. Honeysuckle and black bryony sprawl over the hedges by the track. Where you cross a stream, meadowsweet is flourishing and a few alder trees line the course of the stream. A footpath sign points back up the way we have come. Ahead a metalled road continues, up to the barn conversions at Auton Court, where rare cuckoo pint is abundant at the foot of the walls and along the banks. After a few more twists and turns we meet the lane to Easton; we turn right. There is dogwood in the hedge, which is conspicuous by its red stems. Ropes of the reddening berries of black bryony climb the hedges in the autumn, and clumps of stinking iris grow on the banks. Look out for an attractive view, through the gateway on the right.

At Easton Farm turn left and almost immediately right, following a footpath sign. The path turns right, under a spreading horse-chestnut tree and left, to follow the hedge on your right.

At the top of the slope is a cross-roads of paths. This is where you meet the short-cut route. You could go straight on to take a short-cut back to Kingsbridge. Otherwise, turn left and you find yourself in a sunken lane, arched over with blackthorn and hazel. Primroses line some of the shaded banks. As you come out of the green gloom, by a mass of Alexanders, turn right onto the lane. Stop to admire the view of West Alvington and Kingsbridge, down to the right where all valleys meet. You can walk to West Alvington either down the lane, past the little copse, where wood anemones blow in spring, or over the stone stile at the top of the hill and down the pasture field. From the field you can see the tall beeches of the copse on your left. A buzzard is often wheeling over the valley. In the valley bottom are the remains of an old hedge-bank, with a turkey oak, a sycamore and two mature hazel trees. Cross the stream, by an ancient English oak and climb up and to the left to emerge onto a lane. This lane, lined with old cottages and walls with red valerian and pellitory of the wall growing out of them, leads up to the main road, by West Alvington School. Carefully cross the road and take a walk around the fine church and its churchyard. Over the porch is a sculpture of Bishop Hugh of Lincoln feeding a swan, it is in memory of Hugh Lethbridge, a much-loved vicar of the parish. In the churchyard is a mound of bramble smothered in old man's beard and Russian vine; a paradise for nesting blackbirds and thrushes, that use the grave stones as anvils, on which to break snails' shells.

Continue along the high pavement above the main road for 100 metres. Turn off left at the footpath sign, by the telephone box. This path has rare and common cuckoo-pint, winter heliotrope, Alexanders and balm-leaved figwort along its zig-zag course. It leads into West Alvington Wood. Climb the big stile, under the dark holly trees. Giant oaks, chestnuts and beeches soar above you. The hazel bushes, beloved of dormice, grow beneath and the woodland floor is covered by green tussocks of great woodrush. In spring, bluebells push through the crunchy drifts of fallen leaves and blackcaps, robins, wrens, blackbirds and thrushes sing. Jays collect acorns in the autumn. Great spotted woodpeckers nest and forage on the older, rotting branches. The path winds down through the wood, veering off to the left at the bottom, where you emerge onto another pretty lane.

Walk north along the lane for about half a mile. There are two fine oaks on the right, a South Devon elm that has escaped Dutch elm disease on the left and two more oaks near the entrance to Home Farm. This is another beautiful lane for flowers; meadowsweet, shining cranesbill, bugle, primrose, lesser celandine, birdseye speedwell, red campion, ground ivy, foxglove and hedge bedstraw - all have their season. Especially in the autumn, skylarks, yellowhammers and finches feed in the stubble or set aside fields either side of the lane.

When you reach the main road, turn right and almost immediately take the footpath to your right, over a stile into a long triangular field. The path follows the right hand hedge, towards the wind-pruned beech trees by Norton Farm. Here you continue through the old orchard, where blackbirds, redwing and fieldfares come to feast on windfall apples in the late autumn and winter. Go between the two barns and follow the concrete track up the ridge until, at the crest of a knoll, you have a glorious view over Kingsbridge.

Heading towards the estuary, keep the clump of trees on your left, and climb the stile in the south-east corner of the field. Follow the hedge on your left and at its end, climb the stile. Walk across the field for about 100 metres to a gate. Turn right, beside the old railway track, which is now converted into well-kept allotments, and turn left, over the old railway bridge, built in 1893.

You are now in Hurrell Road heading straight towards the spire of St.Edmund's church. H.G.Hurrell was a naturalist of national and international renown, who lived at Wrangaton, near Ivybridge and kept 'tame but free' otters, Atlanta the grey seal and pine martins in his garden.

At the bend carry straight on down a flight of steps and across the main road to the path that leads down under hazel, laurel, grey alder and tall poplars. To the left, one of the strips of garden belonged to George Montagu and his mistress, Eliza Dorville. It was probably here that they kept their aviaries with captive cirl buntings, cuckoos, waterfowl, Montagu's harrier, a heron and a chough.

Walk up the path and climb the steps to St. Edmunds church and the car park.

6. SLAPTON and TORCROSS
Lanes, lakes, sea and shingle
Length: Walk A 3 miles, Walk B 8 miles.
Parking on the seafront car park (with toilets) half way along Slapton Line,
near the turn-off to Slapton, and at Torcross, by the tank.

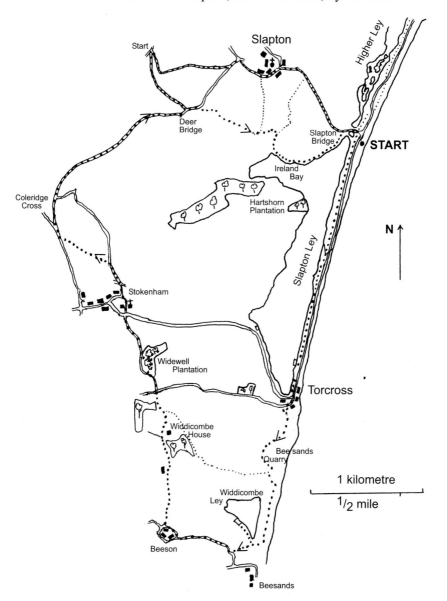

Walk A

From the car park, where you may see gulls, cormorants and perhaps gannets diving offshore, walk back to Slapton Bridge. Pause here for five or ten minutes. Slapton Bridge gives a grandstand view of the passing wildlife. It is probably the best place to see a Cetti's warbler. This little, dark, chocolate brown bird, is a rarity. It flits through the reeds or bushes and its short, explosively loud song is said to be the inspiration for the opening bars of Mozart's 'Eine Kleine Nacht Music'. Unlike most warblers, it stays throughout the year. In summer reed warblers come from Africa to nest in the swaying reeds. All day and all night, from the reed jungle, comes the rasping song of the males. They are known locally as 'Torcross nightingales'. Every so often you will see one fly across the waterway, between the waving walls of reed.

In winter, you may see a water-rail, stalking along the edge of the waterway, jabbing among the ragged remains of the water plants with its long, scimitar bill. If you are really early in the morning, you may be lucky enough to see an otter or a mink, both of which regularly pass beneath the bridge at night.

Willow bushes and fennel plants sprout by the roadside. Down by the water are two grasses. The common reed is the tallest and dominates, especially in the Higher Ley. Its feathery heads do not come into flower until August. It looses its leaves in winter. Growing by it, often closer to the edge, is the shorter, purple headed, reed-grass. Reed-grass flowers from June and, although its leaves become withered and creamy-brown, they remain all winter.

Walk on up the road to the village of Slapton. As you enter the village, the Field Studies Centre is the first building on your right. You can get the latest information on recent sightings and details of guided walks from here. They provide a wonderful variety of residential courses throughout the year.

Keep straight on by the Post Office and through this attractive old village, not turning right where the main road bends sharply. On the walls look out for the pink, red or white flowers of red valerian, and the trailing bellflowers: the bright violet blue bells of *Campanula portenschlagiana* and the pale blue stars of *Campanula porscharskyana*. As you begin to climb again, the road cuts through the bed-rock, New Red Sandstone. This desert deposit used to lie as a thick strata over all the Devonian slates. It has been eroded away from most of the South Hams but around Slapton an outlier remains. After the housing estate on the left, you come to Town's End Cross. Take the left turn and, in a short distance, fork right. The lane here is a picture. Alexanders and greater stitchwort dominate some stretches in the spring. Soon, on the left, is a barn where a pair of little owls roost. Devon farmers call these 'day owls', as they are often active in the day especially early and late, searching for beetles and other insects. The lane descends steeply to an old barn and a post-box. Fine beech trees overhang the lane. Turn sharply left here. On your right is a wide marsh, filled with a thick growth of hemlock water-dropwort and meadow-sweet. On your left. the purple flowers of honesty, a garden escape, bloom in the spring and later their seed heads shine like silver coins. The line of tall trees on your right are aspens, the leaves trembling on the silvery branches in the slightest breeze. From the marshy ditch beside the lane water horsetails grow and patches of kingcups - marsh marigold. In winter this is a haunt for small flocks of teal.

You join another lane, at Deer Bridge. Small trout hang in the clear water here, flickering their tails to hold themselves against the current. Turn left along the lane and immediately right, down a footpath. Pussy willow bushes grow in the marsh to your right and, among the reeds and reed-grass, great clumps of tussock sedge, sometimes six feet tall. Following the route of this old carriageway, you see beautifully built stone gateways and mossy banks with ancient beeches and oaks overhanging the pathway. Before you emerge into the open, there is an old aspen growing on the right of the path and an even older oak on the left. Now, a boardwalk takes you across the marsh, by curving heads of pond sedge, more tussock sedge, yellow iris, meadowsweet and purple loosetrife. The pussy willow bushes are rich in insect life; you may see clusters of lackey moth caterpillars protected by a silken web. In late summer and through the winter, parties of tits, including longtails, flit through the bushes. Chiffchaffs sing from them in early spring. Some of the old pussy willow branches have rotted and have fallen into the peaty water. Water horsetail stems and fronds of lady fern grow from the black swamp, just as their ancestors grew, a hundred feet high, in the swamps of the Carboniferous - 'coal age' - forest. The boardwalk eventually joins a path, where you turn right, under a canopy of sycamore, oak, sweet chestnut and hazel. The path curves to the left and you have glimpses over the marsh, where a phalanx of reed maces rise from the bed of common reed. In May the maces are green, with a yellow pollen-spike above them. Through the summer they are brown and by late autumn, hoary with down flying off like star-dust. A causeway, lined with a few old poplars, leads across the marsh, but it is a closed part of the reserve.

On the left is a disused quarry. A blackcap often sings here, with the robins and wrens, from the undergrowth, while the reed warblers churr away in the great reed-bed of Ireland Bay. Across the bay are coots, often a flock of Canada geese and perhaps a few great crested grebes, their heads held high on long white necks and adorned with chestnut ruff and black crest. On the raft moored in the bay, cormorants stand after their fish meal. Eel, rudd or roach, perch or pike are all on the menu. The pike, 'killers from the egg', are predators on the other fish, on their own kind and on young coot, moorhen, grebes and ducklings.

The path continues through more stone pillars, by the shore of the ley, over raised walkways and up and down the banks, by spikey clumps of butchers' broom. As you look at the plants, you will notice the damselflies, mostly blue, or blue-tailed with a few, slightly larger, red ones by the water's edge. These have all hatched from larvae that have lived under water for a year and now have a brief life as beautiful, winged insects. The bigger dragonflies, especially the black-tailed skimmers, with steely blue bodies, tipped with black. fly low over the water and perch on the stones at the water's edge.

Just before you leave the waterside, there is a big stand of lesser reed-mace, extending out into the water. This has narrower leaves and a thinner mace that the common reed-mace.

There is a short stretch of path through bushes and trees - an excellent stretch to listen for warblers - before you come out by the fishing hut. The clearing is good for butterflies, speckled woods in the shade, red admirals basking on late ivy blossom and holly blues flickering around the taller ivy leaves earlier in the year. Near the hut there is an interpretive board, a blackboard with recent sightings chalked up and rowing boats which authorised fishermen can hire from the Field Centre. All the fish, even the monster pike, have to be returned to the ley, after they have been caught and weighed.

Climb up to the road and pause again as you cross the bridge and return to the car park. The walk finishes here but there is another, longer walk to try another day.

Walk B

Walk B begins at the same car park on the shingle ridge. Nearby is the memorial which records the thanks of the American forces to the people of the South Hams. Walk into Torcross on the path between the road and the Lower Ley - the backslope - or along the shingle ridge.

For about two thousand years, the waves, like a tireless, magic broom, have been pushing the shingle slowly but relentlessly inland. The backslope has been longest colonised by plants. Before the road was built, in the nineteenth century, cattle or sheep would have grazed the backslope, without them some form of cutting is necessary if all the backslope is not to be colonised by bushes and eventually scrub woodland. At present, grasses are dominant, especially the fine-leaved, red fescue. Sea radish, a tall, bushy plant, with masses of pale-yellow flowers and a rosette of tough, ragged leaves, is very common, although nationally it is scarce. The knobbly seed-pods attract flocks of greenfinches in the autumn and winter. Stonechats, flicking their wings and tails, often perch on the tops of bushes and radishes.

Out over the ley, from March until the end of October, flocks of the swallow tribe hunt for insects - midges to damsel flies and dragonflies - millions of them.

35

Sand martins are the first to arrive with swallows following in early April. House martins come later in the month and the black, sickle-winged swifts at the beginning of May. They sometimes gather in thousands, skimming the surface or high overhead. The swifts are the first to leave in August and the house martins, generally the last, in October. Occasional swallows or house martins, who 'missed the flight' are even seen in mid-winter.

Cormorants, often with wings outstretched, rest on the rafts, specially put out for them. Herons nest in Hartshorn Plantation. Out on the water will be white gulls, black coots, mallard, perhaps tufted and pochard duck and a few great crested grebes, with their long, pale necks.

As you approach Torcross, pale, blue-flowered chickory plants grow along the roadside. Amongst the grasses grow yellow toadflax, mugwort and its uncommon, aromatic relative wormwood. If you carefully cross the road to explore the shingle between the road and the sea, you find the pebbles have been smoothed and graded by the sea. Most are flint, brought in from an offshore bank but there are also Devon slate, schist and even granite pebbles, washed down from Dartmoor by the River Dart. Along the tide line are decaying seaweeds, shells and all kinds of flotsam and jetsam, hints of earlier and other creation. The greyish lobes, like seaweed, are colonies of animals - sea mats. Other sea mats encrust the fronds of seaweeds.

The commonest shells are trough shells - oval and thick. The biggest of the snail-like, single shelled molluscs is the whelk. Their clusters of papery egg-cases, similar to a ball of bubble-wrap, are often in the tide-line. Much smaller, shiny, globular 'snail' shells, with a ring of dark marks around the top, are necklace shells. These, bore holes into other shells and eat the mollusc inside. The cuttlefish, whose 'bones' are washed up along the tide line, is a swimming mollusc.

Out of the bare shingle shoot the colonising plants. Where the shingle is building up, sea spurge and sand couch grass are pioneers. The splendid yellow-horned poppy, with grey foliage, yellow flowers and seed-pods like cows' horns, grows especially on shingle where there has been recent erosion. There are a very few plants of sea holly and sea kale, springing from the bare shingle. These plants are succeeded by many more - sea campion, sea pink, buckshorn plantain, restharrow, birdsfoot trefoil and the blue

Horned poppy

36

spikes of viper's bugloss. From May to August the shingle bank is ablaze with colour.

In winter the waves roar as they sweep the shingle up the shore and sea-birds battle against the wind. Henry Williamson loved this shore on a windy day.

When you reach the car park, visit the hide. You may see a pair of handsome great crested grebes displaying. They build a raft of vegetation anchored to the reed stems, well away from the shore, for their nest. After the young have hatched, the parents carry them on their backs. Further along the road is an open beach at the corner of the ley, where the tables are turned and the birds come to look at us. With the mallard and assorted hybrids between domestic and mallard ducks, are coots, moorhens and swans. An attractive information panel illustrates the ecology of the ley.

Take the lane by the public toilets and follow the footpath sign up the steep steps to the left. Turn right at the top and then left. Here you can admire the view over the Ley. The footpath continues until it comes out on a grassy meadow and

Torcross and Slapton Ley

then skirts a huge, disused slate quarry. As the path descends steeply, there is a view down over Widdicombe Ley to Start Point lighthouse in the distance. Walk between the shore and the ley to the end of the ley, where there is a car parking area. From here a path turns inland, by the southern side of the ley to the birdwatching hide. This is the Mike Rogers hide, named in gratitude to the farmer who has given the land for the hide. From the hide are good views of Canada geese, ducks (gadwall and shoveler are regulars here) and coots and great crested grebes. Reed and sedge warblers nest around the ley. Retrace your steps for about two hundred yards and a public footpath climbs the hill to meet the lane to the hamlet of Beeson. This is an attractive little hamlet, with red valerian growing on the old stone walls. In summer many pairs of house martins nest under the eaves of some of the houses. Take the track northwards to Widdicombe. A footpath continues straight on, climbing up a grassy field with woodland on your right. At the top of the slope there is the remains of a line of old sycamore trees which have some beautiful and unusual species of lichen. From the footpath there are glimpses of Widdicombe House, a fine, elegant building. Keep to the footpath, which continues through the grounds until it comes out into a pasture field. Go down this sloping field to the stile onto the lane, at a T junction. The lane takes you down to Widewell Plantation. This is a delightful, small wood, carpeted with bluebells in April and May. The owners have very kindly opened the wood to the public. Go in at the first entrance on the right and follow the path as it makes a long, hair-pin bend through the wood, coming back out on the lane at the bottom of the hill. In a few hundred metres, the lane meets the main road, on the edge of the village of Stokenham. Cross the road to the Church House Inn.

Follow the lane past the impressive church tower. At the left hand bend, turn right and soon right again to head uphill out of the village. In about 100 metres a footpath leads left across the fields, up to Coleridge Cross. Larks sing overhead.

Turn right along the lane, which has views down the valley to Slapton and along the coast towards Dartmouth. On a spur, before the lane falls steeply down to Deer Bridge, is the remains of an iron age fort, now called 'The Castle'. Caches of wave-rounded pebbles, brought from the beach, have been found by the earthen embankment, sling stones, for use two thousand years ago. In spring, the hedgebanks either side of the lane, where it slopes down to Deer Bridge, are splashed with the pale yellow and gold blossoms of primroses and celandines. By mid-April they are blue with bluebells and before May is out the bracken towers on either side. By autumn, tall clumps of dingy-pink hemp agrimony attract the butterflies.

After Deer Bridge, take the path to the right, down the old carriage-way, across the marshes by board-walk and along the shore of the ley until you arrive back at Slapton Bridge. Time to stand and stare, looking for the elusive otter.

7. MODBURY
Runaway Lane, Cottlass, Rogues' Roost, Butland and Wastor Woods,
Shearlangstone, Hunts Cross, Little Modbury and Swanbridge Mill
Walk A 3 miles, Walk B 7 miles.
Park in the main Modbury car park at Poundwell Meadow,
near the health centre.

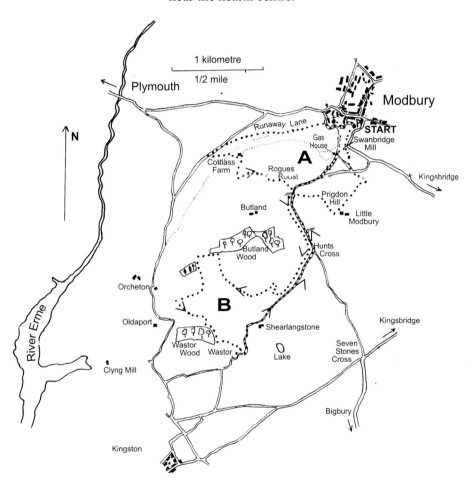

Walk A
Leave the car park, by Modbury Health Centre, as if you are going into the
town but turn left, up the lane that leads towards the church. As the lane becomes
steeper and overhung with branches, in springtime the banks are white with

ramsons. Turn right, where the lane forks and climb up the steps into the churchyard, admiring the old building and the flowers that thrive in God's acre.

Having circled the church, leave by the gate in the south-west corner and turn right along Vicarage Lane. Back in the Nineteenth century, the vicar, George Clarke Green, had cobbles laid. The cobbles are still there by a flowery bank beneath an old beech hedge.

After 100 metres, you turn left, either following the footpath sign into the field or the track immediately after. We will take the track, Runaway Lane, by which, according to legend, the Royalists ran away after the Battle of Modbury, in 1643. The first part of the lane is open and butterflies often flounce and sunbathe here. The hedge has a rich variety of tree species, including field maple, which together with sycamore, ash, elder and dogwood are the only common species with buds opposite each other, in pairs. On the right a patch of the invasive alien, winter heliotrope is spreading. Soon the green lane dips down, beween steep banks, cloaked in mosses, and ferns. The most common moss is dark green, with capsules on nodding stalks, which give it the name of 'swans' neck moss'. Overhead, huge beech trees tower, forming a translucent green canopy in summer. Beech leaves and beech-mast, the prickly-husked nuts, are strewn on the path. At the bottom of the slope, a wooden bridge takes you across a stream. Liverworts spread over the bare clay of the stream sides, by a miniature waterfall.

Winter heliotrope

The public footpath joins Runaway Lane for this section but soon leaves it again to continue parallel to the lane but nearer to the Ayleston Brook. Runaway Lane used to become very muddy but has now been resurfaced. A tawny owl may rest in the thick ivy on some of the trees, hiding from mobbing songbirds. Beneath the canopy of the larger trees, hazel arches across the track. From January, the lambstail catkins hang down, sending golden clouds of pollen, to pollinate the tiny red flowers. By August you can see next year's catkins already formed, as well as the swelling hazel nuts. Throughout the autumn, squirrels, dormice and wood-mice will feed on them and the tawny owls will watch by night for the wood-mice scampering below.

Among the coppiced hazel are a few spindleberry bushes, easily identified by the green stems of last year's growth, and the pink globular berries. There is a badger's sett in the bank, easily spotted because of the huge piles of spoil dug out. Elder trees thrive in the nitrogen-rich soil. Alder trees line the meandering brook. As Runaway Lane begins to climb, you have views across the valley and downstream towards where the Ayleston Brook joins the River Erme at Oldaport. Soon you meet the road, where you turn left and left again in about 200 metres, down the track that leads to Cottlass. The public footpath meets this track, just before it crosses the brook. Cross the brook and go past the well-kept buildings at Cottlass. Both herons and little egrets fish in the brook here. There is a short-cut back to Modbury by taking the old track off to the left but we continue uphill; the path zig-zags to ease the gradient. There are a number of mature ash trees growing up from the hedgebank, some cloaked in ivy. On dead ash wood grow black fungi known as cramp balls (they have been used as a cure for rheumatism) or King Alfred's cakes - too long in the oven!

Near the top of the hill are panoramic views to the north. By two gates on the left, these views are especially good. Buzzards soar over the valley here, making their mewing cries. The top of this hill is known as Rogues' Roost and perhaps highwaymen identified likely looking vehicles coming along the road from Plymouth. You can see Edmeston, with Ermington Wood just cresting the hill behind. On the skyline is an ancient ridgeway, marked by a broken line of Scots pines. Modbury town is to the right and far beyond rise Dartmoor and Brent Hill.

Where gates open onto the wide cereal fields of the high plateau, I have seen foxes making their way across the fields and along the rabbit rich hedges, hares also. The track comes out on the lane between Modbury and Kingston, near the top of Prigdon Hill.

Cross the lane and climb the steps in the hedge bank to climb the stiles. This hill, Prigdon Hill, gives the best views of Modbury. The path crosses the field, rising to meet the hedge on your right.

The path turns right towards Little Modbury farm and then left downhill to meet the old drovers' track, which turns left again, to meet the lane at a cross-ways. Cross the lane to take the less used way and in about 50 metres, on the right, a footpath crosses the hedge into a pasture field, down which winds the Ayleston Brook. All the common buttercups grow in this meadow; lesser celandines, in the spring, the broad-leaved, creeping buttercups, at the foot of the hedges, bulbous buttercups, with their down-turned sepals, on the better drained banks and many meadow buttercups, in the meadow, taller than all the rest. Ayleston Brook is a clean stream. Mayfly larvae, freshwater shrimps, water hoglice, flatworms and leeches live under the stones and among the weed. On the stones from the stream bed are caddis-fly larva and freshwater limpets. Children fishing here have caught stone loaches, minnows and sticklebacks, miller's thumbs and eels. Early in the morning, you may disturb a grey heron searching for the eels for his breakfast.

Cross the brook by the slab bridge and the path goes up to the corner of the field, over a stone stile to Swanbridge Mill. Bear right, with the stream on your right, fringed with tall hemlock water-dropwort, water-figwort and meadowsweet. You may see slender, blue damselflies or beautiful demoiselle damselflies, shining metallic green or blue, resting on the foliage or fluttering weakly over the stream. Soon you reach a kissing gate and the car park, where we began.

Walk B

From the health centre car park, walk away from the town, through the kissing gate and along the path. On your left is the stream with its fringe of water-loving plants, on your right the pasture field, sloping up to a Devon hedge bank, crowned with hazel bushes, and the church beyond on the skyline. When you reach Swanbridge Mill, take the right hand fork in the path. By this path, the big, rhubarb-like leaves of butterbur grow near the stream and, in February and March, the pink flower spikes rise, very similar to its alien relative the winter heliotrope. Long ago country people wrapped their pats of butter in the cool leaves of butterbur. Looking over to the left, the oak branches spread over the buttercup meadow and swallows swoop and chatter all summer long .

Where the path meets the lane is a group of buildings, including a tall, brick chimney. This used to be Modbury's gas works, which lit the streets of Modbury from 1865 to 1932, when electricity arrived.

Turn left up the lane to climb a steep hill. Near the top, where the lane joins another, are the remains of an old toll-house for the turnpike road to Kingston. Continue up the hill until reaching the stone pillars by the entrance drive to Butland. Follow the new permissive bridle path, which John Coyte, the farmer at Butland, has allowed on his land. On a clear day there are spectacular views over the South Hams. Go through the gate to the left of the stone pillars and follow the hedge along to the left, parallel to the road. To the right is Butland Farm, its farm pond, where Canada geese nest, and the plantation of Douglas fir and larch, over which buzzards wheel.

The path follows the hedge and lane, past Hunts Cross, for about half a mile. Then it turns right and zig-zags round a sharp bend. Ash is dominant in the hedgerow. The path stays beside the hedge that heads westward and slowly bends right until it is going north. Some clumps of coppiced ash have been allowed to grow into trees and chaffinches and yellowhammers use them as song posts. Rabbits have dug their warrens into the hedge banks. Above the rippling cereal fields, larks sing - specks against the blue sky.

Ahead, the fields roll down, over the spur of rectangular fields beyond Great Orcheton Farm and the spur of green pasture at Oldaport, to the marshes of the Erme estuary. Woodland climbs the valley sides. Beyond the Erme valley, the village of Holbeton, and its spired church, peep out from between wooded hills.

As you continue straight on, through one of the three gates where hedges meet, the view north, over Ermington Wood to Dartmoor, appears over the brow of the hill. Below you is Butland Wood. The path goes downhill to the wood, where are coppiced hazel bushes, bramble and an old crab apple, hung with leafy and bearded lichens. Turn left along the edge of the wood and left again at the next hedge, to climb back up the hill, past a small plantation of Sitka spruce. At the top of the hill, you are looking southwards, across the valley of Wastor Brook to Wastor Wood. Where the hedge turns sharply left, you turn right, through a gate into a huge pasture field sloping down into the valley. Our route goes round two sides of this field. Head downhill, towards the Erme estuary, keeping the hedge on your right. When you meet the next hedge, turn left, downhill again, towards Wastor Wood. At the bottom of the slope the fence bends left, where a strip of mixed woodland has been planted in the valley bottom. Just after the line of silvery blue Sitka spruce, a muddy track zigzags down to the stream, by sweet chestnut, cherry and pussy willows buzzing with bees at Eastertime.

Cross the stream and this is an idyllic spot for a picnic. Grey wagtails - easily recognised by their grey backs and bright yellow bellies - come down to the water's edge, snapping up midges and stoneflies and wagging their long tails. Old oak trees lean over the path, mosses and polypody ferns growing from their knotted branches. Around the holly trees, growing by the stream, holly blue butterflies flicker in early spring, choosing where to lay their eggs. Ladies smock grows in the wet meadow by the brook and orange-tip butterflies settle, laying their tiny orange eggs, at the base of the flowers. Alder trees line the brook and clumps of foxgloves spear up from the hedgebank.

The path continues across the meadow, keeping the stream on your left and Wastor Wood on your right. The wood has many old oaks climbing the steep slope; under them hazel coppice, festooned with honeysuckle, provides cover for the blackcaps, returning from North Africa. They sing so beautifully - like operatic robins, only a little less dramatic than the nightingale. Come to Wastor Wood on a spring morning to hear a concert of birdsong. The brook comes close to the path again and, by a little waterfall, golden saxifrage spreads its gold and green carpet. Just before you leave the wood, by an old gateway, there is an ancient ash tree, on the right, with holes and crevices, from which you can imagine creatures peering out at you.

In about 100 metres, turn left, through a gap in the hedge, to follow the brook across another wet, flowery meadow and into a track leading under tall trees to the lane where it crosses Wastor Brook. The little bridge over the brook is beautifully decorated with mosses and hartstongue fern.

Turn left, over the bridge and up the lane towards Shearlangstone. The lane is a picture, the banks are starred white with wild strawberry flowers and greater stitchwort, dappled blue by sweet violets and green alkanet and showered with pink confetti by herb Robert, shining cranesbill and red campion. Climb up past the hamlet of Shearlangstone and follow the lane for nearly a mile, climbing up to Hunts Cross. Turn left until you find yourself back at the entrance to Butland Farm. Retrace your steps down the lane to Gas House and Swanbridge Mill and follow the path by the stream back to the health centre car park.

8. EAST PRAWLE,

Coastal walk to Prawle Point and Maceley Cove and inland to Goodshelter and West Prawle Wood.

Distance: 8 miles.

Park by The Green in East Prawle village.

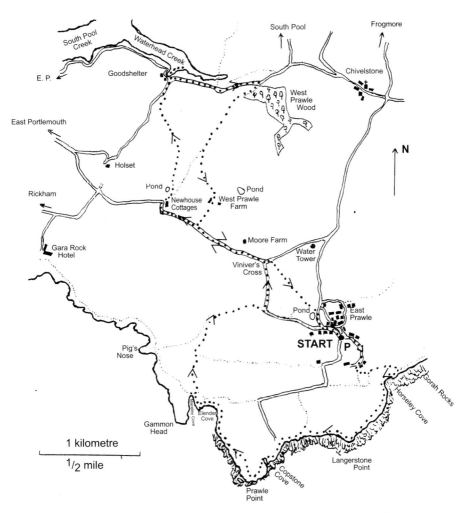

Leave the car park at Prawle Green by the narrow lane at the south-east corner. The lane is bounded by a wall with English stonecrop, fern-grass and thyme-leaved sandwort growing on it. Little Robin, a close relative of herb Robert also grows on the stony banks round Prawle. The lane curves to the right, giving views out over Lannacombe Bay to Peartree Point. When you reach a cluster of houses, the lane peters out. Take the footpath to the left and in about 100 metres climb over the wall-stile into the steeply-sloping pasture field. Pause to admire the view down to the wave-cut, rocky platform at Horseley Cove, covered by the sea at each high tide. To the left you can see the rocky bluffs, remains of cliffs formed by the sea before the last ice age, when sea-level was higher. Between the old cliff-line and the new, is an apron of land, tilled for early crops. This was formed by great mud-slides towards the end on the last ice age, about ten thousand years ago. While you look at the geological story laid out below, you might well hear a cirl bunting and see them in the bushes nearby.

The path descends the steep field and over a wall-stile at the bottom. Turn left down the sunken way, by the copse on your left, and continue, through the gate and by the hedge, straight ahead. A western species, the narrow-leaved everlasting

pea, sprawls over this hedge and along the cliff-top with the bloody cranesbill. You can go rock-pooling and shell-collecting down on the beach at Horseley Cove or immediately turn right along the cliff top to

East Prawle, Horseley Cove

follow the coast path round to Prawle Point. Out on the seaweeds of the cove there are oystercatchers, cracking open limpets. Other waders - turnstones, curlew, whimbrel, redshank and grey plover rest here, especially at migration times.

By the path, where it rounds Sharpers Head and Langerstone Point, is a prolific spread of bloody cranesbill, thrift, sea campion, kidney vetch, and birdsfoot trefoil. There also patches of the rarer, hairy birdsfoot trefoil. In the fields are many interesting 'weeds' which have become generally uncommon, because of herbicides. In the bushes the rare cirl buntings may be seen. The males have a rattling, repetitive song.

Above, on the rocky inland cliff, crows, ravens, kestrels or peregrines may be perched, surveying all that moves, including us. I have seen a kestrel catch a great green bush-cricket here. These harmless insects are fairly common in the

South Hams but look quite frightening; two or three inches long, bright green and, in the females' case an ovipositor sticking out behind, like a sword.

Keep to the path near the cliffs and at Copstone Cove, look down at the rocks. With a few oystercatchers and turnstones, there may be some purple sandpipers, which have yellow legs, rather than the orange ones of the similar sized turnstones or pink legs of the larger, black and white oystercatchers.

There is a stile over the fence here, which leads to a steep path, up between rocky outcrops of the schist rock, to the National Coast Watch lookout at Prawle Point. As well as looking for ships, it is a splendid site to watch out for sea birds. You will see gannets, shags and gulls, and sometimes passing shearwaters and skuas.

From August the leafless mauve spikes of autumn squills speckle the grassland. All the cliff flowers we have seen before grow commonly by the cliff path as it continues westwards. The path from Prawle Point to Gammon Head gives views of some of the most dramatic coastal scenery in the South Hams. The green rock is horneblende schist , a metamorphosed volcanic rock, which weathers into fascinating honeycomb patterns. Round Signalhouse point is the first view of Elender and Maceley Coves, protected by the impressive spur of Gammon Head. Choose a good view above the coves for a stopping place. Ravens and shags nest on the cliffs, kestrels hover over the grassy slopes and often a peregrine streaks by on grey wings. Spring squill and bloody cranesbill are abundant by the clifftop. If you want to swim, there is a steep path down to the sandy beach far below.

The coast path continues on to Gara Rock Hotel and beyond to East Portlemouth but our route turns inland above Maceley Cove. Turn right and, in

Prawle - Elender Cove and Maceley Cove

about a hundred metres, left, to climb northwards along the side of the tongue-shaped field that ends above Maceley Cove. At the top of the climb, where a farm track leads off to the right, take the narrow path that goes straight on. You have views of Bolt Head on the far side of the Salcombe Estuary. Soon you come into a steep pasture field in Pig's Nose valley. Forests of nodding thistles grow here, with big, beautiful, sweet-scented flowerheads. They are very attractive to insects.

The path leads into the valley. Stunted trees and thorn scrub shelter the path and migrant warblers, goldcrests and firecrests feed in the thick cover. In late summer the dusty pink flowers of hemp agrimony and ripening blackberries have red admiral butterflies fluttering around.

Carry on up the Pig's Nose Valley path. The upper part is called Merrymoor Lane. Where it meets the metalled lane, at a right angle turn, you can continue along the lane into Prawle to finish the walk at this stage, but the walk continues by turning left along the lane to Viniver's Cross. There are hedges of hawthorn and blackthorn, with some elder, ash, privet and hazel. In the spring it is lined with Alexanders. In late summer there are many tall patches of hemp agrimony, which make this lane particularly attractive for butterflies.

At Viniver's Cross turn left along the road; you have good views north across the South Hams countryside to Dartmoor. The four common umbellifers, with flowerheads shaped like umbrellas, all grow along this road. First, in March and April, the yellow-green flowered, Alexanders. In April and early May, cow parsley follows, a little later rough chervil, and finally hogweed, the big, hairy one. The tall, tufted grass along the verge is reed fescue, a speciality of South Hams lanes near the sea.

Just past the turning to West Prawle house and farm, the hedge is of stunted elms. In winter, the fields on either side may have flocks of lapwings and golden plover, as well as rooks and jackdaws. At the sharp bend to the right, the round leaves of winter heliotrope are spreading. In December and January, its almond scented, mauve flower spikes spring up by the new leaves.

After Newhouse Cottages, take the footpath off to the right. Immediately on your right, honesty grows on the bank. In April the tall, branched stems are bright with purple flowers. Honesty is a traditional cottage garden flower often naturalised near hamlets and villages.

After 100 metres down the bridle track, lined with elm trees, go through the little gate on the left and walk down to the pond on your left.

Keeping the pond on your left, follow the stream down the valley. By the stream is a line of very old alder trees. Further down the stream, there is more hazel and pussy willow. The valley is a sheep-walk. Meadow and bulbous buttercups sway among the grasses and tall thistles tower above. The paler flowered are creeping thistles and the dark purple ones, with the sharp spikey leaves, are spear thistles. Both attract butterflies, including painted ladies, which lay their eggs on the thistles. Meadow brown butterflies are the commonest over the grassland in mid-summer.

Along the stream, below the hedgebank foxgloves tower in June. The path passes stands of stinging nettles, and on these you may find the caterpillars of small tortoiseshell, peacock and red admiral butterflies.

Shortly before a line of South Devon elms, coming down to the stream from the left of the valley, veer to the right, contouring along the right hand side of the valley, through some gorse scrub. Aim for the right hand end of a line of trees several hundred metres ahead - ashes and sycamore - where there is a gate in the hedge. Celandines grow best on south-facing banks and in the short grass below the line of ash trees, the yellow flowers of the celandines are a picture from February until April. By May the celandines have withered away; the red spikes of sheep's sorrel and the butter-yellow meadow buttercups have taken their place among the grasses. Hawkbits and catsear, in the dandelion family, follow by July. Go through the little gate as directed by the yellow footpath arrow and down the path between low banks. Cross a stile and down an even steeper slope. You pass under an arch of holly, spindleberry and Russian vine, where hartstongue and soft shield ferns and wall pennywort dominate, to meet a narrow lane.

Turn right along the lane. Pass beneath a big elm and meet the main South Pool to East Portlemouth lane at a steep hairpin. You can go down to where the lane fords the creek. From Goodshelter Creek, a redshank may fly off, giving a sharp warning call. Out on the mud a few curlew probe with their long, down-curved bills. A little egret, pristine white, may be stalking or dancing up a runnel of shallow water and a heron waiting patiently by deeper water. The pine trees of Gullet Plantation, on the far bank of the creek, are sometimes used by nesting herons.

Retrace your steps to the hairpin bend, bearing left and continue uphill along to Waterhead. Keep to the lane, ignoring the footpaths off to the left. There are glimpses of stepping stones over the creek, the head of Goodshelter Creek and the gunwales of an old boat sticking out of the mud.

Take the Wood Lane bridlepath, on your right, up to West Prawle Wood. A little way up Wood Lane, the bank on the right is clothed in swan's neck moss, one of the commonest woodland mosses. Opposite this bank a path leads off to the left, into the private wood, but we keep to the main track, which leads up and to the right, under an arching conopy of beech. The trunks from which the branches soar are ribbed and fissured and moss creeps over the smooth bark. As you climb higher up the path, oaks begin to replace the beeches. From the banks, broad buckler and male ferns sprout, as well as the more common hartstongue and soft shield ferns, with shiny tussocks of great wood-rush. To the right there is a view down Goodshelter Creek, framed by the canopy of oaks. In spring the woodland flowers - primrose, wood speedwell, red campion, wood sorrel, yellow pimpernel, wood avens, herb Robert, wood sanicle and bluebell -create a rainbow of blossom. The woodland birds - robin, wren, blackcap, blackbird and thrush - sing.

Where the path emerges, above the wood, are views of treeless combes and green domed hills, copses tucked down in the valleys, the grey tower of Chivelstone church, and the rounded water tower at Prawle. To the north you can see the town of Kingsbridge beyond Beacon Plantation - a hilltop clump of trees.

The path goes on between stony, bracken-clad banks. There are 'up-and-over' tracks, worn where badgers cross the path on their nightly patrols. When the bank stops, by a gorse bush, there is a gate off to the left. Follow this track, above a grassy combe. The combe is so steep that the soil creeps downhill, in ripples like flowing water. Patches of gorse grow across the pasture; this is where linnets, yellowhammers and whitethroats nest in summer. Away at the head of the combe is a pond. Continue along the track by foxgloves and a stony bank on your right, topped with a straggling hawthorn hedge.

Bear right, to the buildings of West Prawle, a fascinating mixture of tasteful conversion, modern farm buildings and old ruins. Chaffinches, house sparrows, yellowhammers and collared doves are attracted by the spilt grain around the new barns.

The track leads out to the main road, where you turn left. 100 metres past Viniver's Cross, turn right to follow the straight footpath along the edge of the fields, the old wartime air-fields. Golden plover sitting in these, their spangled golden backs contrasting with the green of the young corn, are a beautiful sight.

The path brings you to the village pond, surrounded by lichen-rich scrub, near High House Farm. Sedge warblers, moorhen and mallard nest here and many rare migrants have been found. In the winter flocks of yellowhammers gather in the bushes, their yellow heads shining against the silvery lichens. By the pond grow osiers, once used for making crab- and lobster-pots. Hemlock water-dropwort grows rampantly around and some winter heliotrope on the bank by the road. In the pond the blue flowered brooklime and other water weeds compete unsuccessfully with parrot's feather weed, a Peruvian invader.

Follow the road back into East Prawle to the car park and refreshment.

9. DARTMOUTH
Gallants Bower, Warfleet, Swannaton, Little Dartmouth, Dancing Beggars,
Combe Rocks and Blackstone Point
Length: 5 miles
Parking along road above Dartmouth Castle (Map ref. SX 886 503) and limited
parking at the end of the lower road by the old battery, (SX 887 503) where
there are refreshments and toilets.

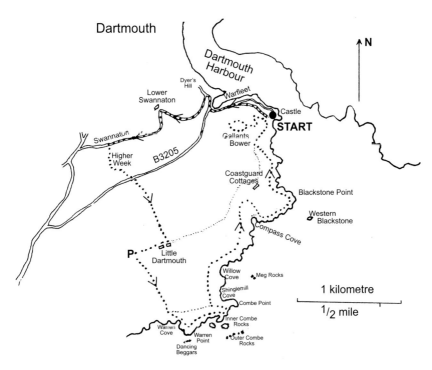

Stand above Dartmouth Castle, looking out over the mouth of the River Dart.
Several old fortifications guard the harbour entrance: the ruins of John Hawley's
14th century castle, the 15th century Castle - an English Heritage site open to the
public - and the 19th century battery, where the cafe is housed. Study the useful
information board opposite the battery cafe, below John Hawley's castle.

Begin by climbing up from the Castle to Gallants Bower, a natural hill used
as a Royalist fort for a short period of the Civil War, in the 1640s. The climb up
to Gallants Bower and the circuit of the top only takes about half an hour and it
sets the whole walk in the context of a birdseye view of the Dart Estuary, the
steep combes, green fields and rugged coast.

From the information board, walk round to the left of Hawley's castle. The steep drop to Castle Cove is on your left and the walls of the old castle on your right. Growing on both rocky slopes is wild cabbage, a rare native which grows commonly around the cliffs near Dartmouth. Also spreading on the banks and verges is winter heliotrope. It is a plant which belongs in the Mediterranean region. Introduced into gardens as a ground cover and for its winter-flowering, almond-scented blooms, it has now naturalised itself. Climb the steps to the higher road, cross it and go through the staggered wooden barrier by the National Trust sign announcing you are entering Gallants Bower. The path zigzags up through a woodland of sycamore trees. Among the ground flora of ivy and bramble, primroses, bluebell, wild strawberry and wood sanicle grow. The path bends to the left and comes out, through a kissing gate, onto the open hillside where the trees have been felled. The flowers are flourishing, as if they had been let out of prison: celandines, primroses and dog's mercury followed by bluebells and red campion, early purple orchids and the forgetmenot blue of green alkanet. Sorrel, foxgloves, wood sage and willow herb continue the procession of flowers.

Climb to the top of the earthen banks, that were the fort, and make a circuit to enjoy the spectacular views. Northwards is Dartmouth, the Royal Naval College and the River Dart. To the left set in a steep combe is Lower Swannaton Farm. Seawards are Blackstone Point and the Western Blackstone and to the left Froward Point and the pointed rocky islet of the Mew Stone.

Make a detour, south-westwards, over the flat, open spur, with patches of bracken, scrub and woodland. The bluebells here are a darker, more intense blue than in the open; from April to June they are a picture. By the path some cream-flowered, climbing corydalis grows, clambering over other plants. Return to the fort and down the zigzag path back to the road.

Turn left along the road, which goes to Warfleet Creek. There is a public space, with seats set down by the water and the remains of two lime kilns, where, two hundred years ago, coal and limestone would have been burnt in layers to provide lime to spread on the fields. The round leaves of winter heliotrope are spreading here.

Bluebell

Bear right, joining the B3205 road. Walk up onto the raised pavement on the left hand side of the road. Down to the right is the bustling waterway of the river. Go on past the Gramercy Tower and then turn left, round the hairpin bend, into Swannaton Road. The road is through suburban Dartmouth. Mind-your-own-business and red valerian are growing on the walls. After a few hundred metres, Swannaton Road turns into a country lane. winding round a combe, where the steep pasture is ribbed by soil-creep. Follow the lane up to Swannaton and turn left along the public footpath, signed just after the last of the buildings. The path skirts the buildings at Week and comes down to the B3205. Turn left for about 20 metres and then take the footpath to the right. This path climbs a hill and meets a major track at Little Dartmouth farm.

Turn right along this track. Notice the ferns on the farm walls - maidenhair spleenwort, polypody and rustyback. Soon you reach the National Trust car park. An information board gives details and a picture of a cirl bunting. Turn left, leaving the car park at the seaward end, where you come onto a path. To your left is a view out to the Mew Stone off Froward Point, and to the daymark tower on the horizon. The path goes down three fields; a blackthorn hedge is on your right. Singing from the top of this hedge may be a cirl bunting, a sage-green and brown bird, with a black bib. At the bottom of the last field, seaside thistle grows. Its slender, purple heads are a picture and attract dozens of butterflies, including immigrant painted ladies and clouded yellows.

Having gone through the gate at the end of the path, don't turn sharp left onto the track which follows the wall but instead take the path straight on towards the sea. This soon veers left through gorse and elder scrub. Some gorse will always be in bloom but in April it is at its golden, coconut-scented best. To the right, you can see across Leonard's Cove, below Stoke Fleming, and down Slapton Sands to the lighthouse on Start Point, about eight miles away.

For a few yards you join the main path beside the fields. Over the field to the left, skylarks sing and, especially in the winter, flocks of linnets feed in the stubble fields. Turn right, off the main path, and continue on the tongue of grass, leading seawards. To your right, on the steep slopes at the head of Warren Cove, wild cabbage grows. On the grassy tongue, leading out towards Warren Point, are musk thistles, rising from rosettes of prickly leaves, their big, purple heads, nodding in the sea breeze. Fiddle docks grow here too - their violin-shaped leaves making them identifiable at any time of year; they are usually only found in Southern Britain, in grassy places by the sea.

Continue following the path, through the gorse, towards the sea. A plaque, fixed on a rock, records that this land around Warren Point was purchased for the National Trust by the Devon Federation of Women's Institutes, in 1970. Growing around the edge of the gorse thickets are celandines, violets and ground ivy in the spring. Heath groundsel, shoots up where the gorse has died back or been burnt. Off Warren Point is a group of black rocks, at high tide only the knobbly tops show, like five heads bobbing among the waves, and they are fancifully called

The Dancing Beggars. Shags often perch on them, shining green in the sun.

The path, edged with bluebells, sorrel, grasses and bracken, winds around Western Combe Cove, through gorse and blackthorn scrub. Combe Rocks soon come into view, where oystercatchers may be piping on the inner rocks. Shelducks rest here; their nest will be in a rabbit burrow above the cove. On the outer rocks shags gather, a fulmar glides by on stiff wings and on the very top of the rocks a pair of great black-backed gulls perch; they always want to be king and queen of the castle, planning their next act of piracy.

Where the path follows the edge of the gorse and there is open grassland to your left, pause. Many of the birds nesting or feeding in the gorse perch on the bushes. Stonechats flicking their wings and tails, cock linnets, with red patches on their breasts, and golden-headed yellowhammers look out over their prickly domain.

After the gorse finishes, there is a rock on the grassy slope, to your right. Walk down through the grass, alive with grasshoppers, click beetles and leaf-hoppers, to the rock. The geological formation along this stretch of coast is called Dartmouth Slate because it was first described here. This particular rock provides shelter, a lovely view and a microcosm of coastal flora; stiff, grey fingers of 'sea ivory' lichen, the round leaves of navelwort, or wall pennywort, the pink stars of English stonecrop, sprawling rock sea-spurrey and tussocks of sea-pink.

Carefully head down towards the cove, until you come to a flight of steps to the slatey beach. This coast, with its coves and caves, provides the background for John Masefield's book 'Jim Davis', an exciting tale of smuggling. At the head of the cove is a cliff of earth and stone. This is called 'head' by geologists; material that flowed over the South Hams ten thousand years ago, as the latest ice age retreated and the surface layers melted each spring.

Return to the isolated rock and, to get a view of Combe Point, follow the raised bank left for about fifty metres. Combe Point, sticking out into the sea, shows the three zones of coastal lichens - a black band around high-tide level, orange-yellow lichens above this and grey lichens, like sea ivory, above them.

Once you have seen Combe Point, head up the slope to your left, keeping the gorse scrub to your right. Aim for the gate near the right-hand end of the stone wall, at the top of the slope. Through the gate are parallel paths, which cross a grassy slope. Both end by a bushy Monterey pine a few hundred metres away. To your right are Willow and Shinglemill Coves. Beyond is a view to Western Blackstone rock, capped with black lichen.

Look at the Monterey pine, it has needles in bunches of three not bunches of two like the Scots pine. Below it, growing in recently disturbed ground is the tallest, smoothest and most poisonous umbellifer, hemlock. In the shallow water, around the pond on your left, is fools' water-cress, another poisonous umbellifer. Keep to the right of the pond and follow the path through the old, stone gate posts and bend right by the thicket of blackthorn. Soon there is a view down to Willow and Shinglemill Coves over a mature turkey oak tree, a species introduced from southern Europe. Before the end of March, the blackthorn is white with blossom - 'blackthorn winter' - and the March winds send the petals spinning like swivelling snow. In mid-summer, whitethroats swear from the safety of the dense, twiggery. Occasionally the male perches on top for a few moments to give his scratchy song; as he sings, the feathers on his throat stick out like a stubbly, white beard. You may also see a family of long-tailed tits, fluttering over the bushes. Early in April they are making their oval nests, camouflaged with lichens, among the spiny blackthorn twigs. By the path stitchwort, red campion, birdseye speedwell and herb Robert make a natural herbaceous border.

Just before the gate which warns of 'Livestock' ahead, old man's beard, our wild clematis, clambers over the thicket. After the gate, take the lower path, which leads into a steep, grassy valley, framed with foxgloves and many elder bushes. Elders are rich in mosses and lichens and are host to a pinkish-brown fungus called, descriptively, Judas' ear. These bushes often grow around badgers' setts.

Take the path leading down the grassy combe to Compass Cove. Over the bushes, honeysuckle scrambles. As the swallows and martins begin their autumn migration, they often gather in hundreds over this valley. At the bottom of the slope, take the path that continues on towards the sea, going down steeply to a rocky platform. This platform was cut by the sea before the last ice ages. A wooden bridge spans a chasm, where the sea washes in and out. Thrift, kidney vetch and birdsfoot trefoil growing on the bare rock, make this scene a picture in early summer. At any time this headland, along to Blackstone Point, is a delightful place. Enjoy the natural rock garden and listen to the sea swell growling in the caves beneath your feet, like the gentle snoring of a sleeping giant.

Scan the sea and the Western Blackstone, for seabirds and basking seals. Search the grassy cliffs behind you for the white umbels of wild carrot, shiny leaves of sea-beet and tall, wild cabbage - a natural vegetable garden.

The path climbs up above Deadman's Cove, through trees and eventually downhill to Dartmouth Castle, where the walk began.

10. START POINT
Coastal paths and lanes to Hallsands, Kellaton, Lannacombe and Mattiscombe.
Length: 6 miles.
Park at the car park near Start Point.

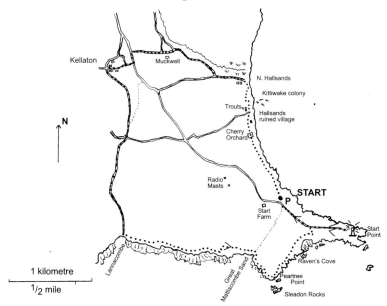

This coastal walk is both beautiful and impressive. Looking north from the car park is a spectacular view. The sea is wearing away the headlands and has built up shingle bars across the bays, creating a straight coastline. Behind the shingle bars, at Hallsands, Beesands and Torcross, are freshwater lagoons, which as they silt up become reed-beds. Take the coastal footpath northwards towards the lost village of Hallsands.

The slopes down to the sea are clothed in gorse and bracken. Over the sea itself wheel herring and black-backed gulls. Often a peregrine falcon glides along the coast, sending parties of cliff-nesting jackdaws flying up in panic. Looking back you see the spur of Start Point, like the tail of a dinosaur laid on the sea, with its lighthouse perched on the end. In April, before the bracken shoots up, its slopes are blue with bluebells.

A few isolated sycamore trees are scattered along the way and old boundary walls show where farmers once cultivated these slopes. A wind-pruned apple tree grows across the path. In spring, violets and celandines grow by the path, later it is flanked by tall foxgloves. Shortly before Hallsands you enter a cherry orchard probably planted more than a century ago. Many suckers are sprouting from the edges of the orchard and the rose-white blossom is a picture in spring. Wall pennywort grows around the gnarled trunks and primroses and red campion by the path.

Coming out from the cherry orchard, on the right is a group of suckering English elms. The mature trees have died of Dutch elm disease but the root system survives and continues to send up suckers. New trees of other species have been planted next to the elms. Ahead is the substantial house which is now Trouts apartments. From March to August you can hear the 'kittiwake' cries from the colony of several hundred kittiwakes which nest on the cliffs below Trouts.

From Trouts is a path leading down to the right to a viewing platform, where you can see the remains of the once thriving village of Hallsands and read about its story. You may also watch the ivory-white kittiwakes sitting on their nests on the vertical cliffs and wheeling out over the sea. A few pairs of our British 'albatross', the fulmar, nest here, gliding by on stiff, outstretched wings.

As you walk back up to Trouts, notice the plants growing by the path; kidney vetch, sea campion and wild carrot. Early in the year the yellow flowers of coltsfoot, a plant that thrives in disturbed soil, pierce the unstable slopes. The garden escape, three-cornered leek, looking like white bluebells, is becoming common along the paths.

Foxglove

Back at Trouts, through the summer, refreshments are available and more information about the remarkable Trout family. At the end of the house is the foundation stone, inscribed: "Patience and Ella Trout O.B.E. Dec. 22nd 1923".

Continue on the coast path and climb the steps to look down on the ruins of the old Bible Christian chapel, now a nesting place for herring gulls. Alexanders, sea radish and tree mallow are prolific by the path. There is a view of the pairs of kittiwakes clustered on their precipitous ledges near the top of the cliff. Kittiwakes are the most attentive partners, greeting each other amorously whenever one returns to the nest from fishing. The cliffs are eroding and may collapse at any time; never leave the main path.

After storms, a submerged forest is sometimes revealed, beneath the shingle beach at North Hallsands. Ancient tree trunks and branches are exposed, set in dark, peaty clay; evidence of the lower sea levels, two thousand years ago when our Iron Age ancestors lived in the South Hams.

Take the lane that goes inland, beside the reed-bed that lies behind the shingle bar. Yellow iris and golden marsh marigolds flower at the edge of the reed-bed. In summer reed and sedge warblers churr from the reeds. Osiers were grown here to provide the withies to make crab and lobster pots, they and pussy willow bushes are spreading and will, one day, overtake the reed-bed. Sweet violets, three-cornered leek and cow parsley grow by the lane. Take the first turn right, at Bridgeway Cross - the sign post says 'Kingsbridge 8' - and continue past the Bickerton Farm Fishery ponds, on your right. You may see Canada geese, moorhens and a kingfisher on these ponds. The lane itself follows the stream and the narrowing strip of reeds. A bittern sometimes winters along this valley.

Keep to the main lane as it begins to climb, passing Muckwell on your left and continuing to climb until you reach the Stokenham to Start Point road. Here turn left for less than a hundred metres and then right, to go downhill between steep banks, with lesser periwinkle and sweet violets, to the attractive little village of Kellaton. At the cross roads, just after the post box, turn left.

Leave the village by this lane between hazel hedges. Some of the hedges down the valley have been recently laid. Among many other hedgerow flowers, early purple orchids flourish on the hedge-banks, Go by the tall copse on your right until you reach Lannacombe Green. Begin to bear left and almost immediately turn right into the cul-de-sac lane to Lannacombe.

This sheltered, flowery lane is excellent for butterflies. The valley bottom, to your left is a thicket of pussy willow. Just before you reach the beach, in about a mile, a pair of cirl buntings often hold a territory in the scrub and rough grassland.

The wall by the car parking area, above the beach, has a lavender dusting of early scurvy grass in March and April and later sea-beet, rock samphire and tree mallows find root nearby. From the beach is safe swimming as the tide comes in and wonderful rock pools to explore at low tide.

Take the coast path through the gate to the left, between blackthorn and gorse bushes. Below is a wave-cut rocky platform, often with a few oystercatchers hammering at limpets. Ahead are grassy fields, rich in flowers, including the strange fiddle dock, with leaves shaped like a violin. Above, to the left, stretches the craggy, prehistoric cliff-line, its steep slopes smothered in golden gorse. Follow the path along the cliff-top but keep inland of the red-topped posts that warn the cliff-edge is falling away. Perched on patches of blackthorn or gorse scrub are stonechats and, in the summer, whitethroats.

There is a bench near the cliff-top, from where you can look into the distance to the left to Peartree Point and to the right to the horse's head arch, off Prawle Point. Below the bench are several conical stacks of stony material. These stacks, called The Pinnacles, have survived the forces of erosion better that the material around them.

After the bench, the path goes up beside a post and rail fence and crosses a stream, fringed with reeds. As you come through a stile after the stream, you have a lovely view of Mattiscombe beach and the fragments of raised-beach around it. Kestrels often hover over the grassland above the beach.

You may take the winding path down to the beach, to bask like seals on the beach. Where a stream makes its way down the steep slope, yellow fleabane, purple loosetrife and tall, pink willow-herb flourish in late summer and are often smothered with butterflies.

Make your way back up to the cliff-top. You can take a short-cut up the valley, back to the car park, but it is worth going on, for the best part of the walk is still to come. To see real basking seals and the most spectacular cliff scenery, continue along the coast path towards Peartree Point.

Once at the point, choose a comfortable, grassy spot by the path and sit down. Look out at the offshore rocks - Sleaden Rocks As the tide ebbs to expose more of the rocky islets, grey Atlantic seals haul themselves out of the water. At first they are dark pelted but as they dry they become lighter. The males have Roman noses. Occasionally they will scratch themselves with a flipper, or stretch, into a banana shape. With a pair of binoculars, you can see their long whiskers and black, soulful eyes. Please do not go down onto the shore to get closer, it will drive them away and deny others this spectacle of domestic bliss.

When you move on, go carefully, enjoying the rock garden of thrift, thyme, English stonecrop and spring and autumn squills, among rocks patterned with lichens. The path climbs to the head of a precipitous gully, Raven's Cove. In March, nearly every year, the ravens come to rebuild their nest with gorse twigs and sheep's wool. Ahead is a curving bay around to Start Point Lighthouse. In winter up to a thousand great black-backed gulls and herring gulls gather on the rocks around this bay. In summer herring gulls and shags nest on the cliff edge and in shaded gullies. The impressive ridge of schist rock descending to Start Point and the lighthouse always reminds me of the armoured back of a Stegosaurus. Green hairstreak butterflies flutter around the gorse scrub on the dinosaur's back. Along its flower-painted sides, silver studded and common blues feed on the nectar of the flowers. Small copper butterflies lay their eggs on the leaves of the rust-red sheep's sorrel. During August the mauve spikes of autumn squill dapple the shorter grassland, where the path reaches the crest of the dorsal ridge. Once over the ridge, the path slopes down to join the road to the lighthouse. Follow the road down to the lighthouse, which may be open for visitors. Look in the tamarisc bushes for migrant warblers, like chiffchaffs or willow warblers. For migrant birds Start is the first or last landfall this side of the English Channel. Wheatears, journeying from North Africa arrive here in March and leave again in the autumn and from here you can watch flocks of swallows, finches and larks, setting out on their journeys. Return up the road until you reach the car park and the wonderful view northwards to Hallsands and beyond, where we began.